ALL THE LIGHT WE CANNOT

An

AUTHORED by Rachel Younger
UPDATED AND REVISED by Aaron Suduiko

COVER DESIGN by Table XI Partners LLC
COVER PHOTO by Olivia Verma and © 2005 GradeSaver, LLC

BOOK DESIGN by Table XI Partners LLC

Published by GradeSaver LLC, www.gradesaver.com

First published in the United States of America by GradeSaver LLC. 2017

ISBN 978-1-60259-746-4

Printed in the United States of America

For other products and additional information please visit http://www.gradesaver.com

Table of Contents

Biography of Anthony Doerr (1973–)

Anthony Doerr is an American author, who was born in 1973 in Cleveland, Ohio. He went to University School, a private boys school, from grades K-12. He then went to Bowdoin College in Brunswick, Maine, where he majored in history, graduating in 1995. He earned his Master in Fine Arts (MFA) from Bowling Green University.

Doerr has published 2 novels, 1 memoir, and 2 collections of short stories. His very first published short story appeared in the *Atlantic* magazine in 2001. He says his biggest influences are writers Anne Carson and Cormac McCarthy. His first published collection of short stories was a book called *The Shell Collector* (2003), and his first novel, *About Grace,* was published in 2004. His memoir, about a year he spent in Rome with his family, was published in 2007.

In 2010, Doerr was awarded the Guggenheim Fellowship, given to those "demonstrating exceptional creative ability in scholarship and the arts." Other writers who have received the fellowship in the past include John Updike, Kurt Vonnegut, and Saul Bellow. That year he released another collection of short stories called *Memory Wall*. Doerr says it took him 10 years to write *All the Light We Cannot See*, which was released in 2014; the novel won the Pulitzer Prize for Fiction in 2015 and was on *The New York Times*' Bestseller List. Aside from writing and publishing books, Doerr has worked as a professor in Boise State University's MFA program in creative writing, and he writes a column on science books for *The Boston Globe*. He also writes for an online publication called *The Morning News*. He was the writer-in-residence for the state of Idaho from 2007 - 2010.

Doerr currently lives in Boise, Idaho with his wife and twin sons.

All the Light We Cannot See Study Guide

All the Light We Cannot See was written by Anthony Doerr in 2014 and was published by Scribner. *All the Light We Cannot See* was Doerr's fifth novel.

The inspiration for the novel came when Doerr was on a trip with a friend whose cell phone broke. He realized how dependent the modern world had become on cell phones, and wanted to write a book in a world where radio had a tremendous amount of power and was the most prominent method of communication. Doerr chose Saint-Malo as a setting after spending some time there and realizing how magical everything in the town was—almost fairytale-like.

All the Light We Cannot See is set during World War II. It follows the stories of a blind French girl whose father works at a Natural History Museum, and of a young German orphan who joins the Nazis as a radio specialist. Their lives cross paths in the most unexpected way as they both struggle though the devastation of war. The novel deals heavily with the themes of light/dark, family loyalty, humanism, and fate.

The novel was both a critical and popular success, spending 118 weeks on *The New York Times* bestseller list for hardcover fiction. Reviewers lauded the book, calling it "[a] masterpiece"(*Financial Times*), "a vastly entertaining feat of storytelling" (*New York Times*) and "so emotionally plangent that some passages bring tears" (Amanda Vaill, *Washington Post*). It received numerous literary awards, including the Pulitzer Prize for Fiction in 2015, an Andrew Carnegie Medal for Fiction in 2015, and the Goodreads Choice Award for Historical Fiction in 2014.

All the Light We Cannot See Summary

All the Light We Cannot See follows the lives of Marie-Laure LeBlanc and Werner Pfennig during a period of time surrounding World War II. The novel alternates between time periods, starting in medias res, during the bombing of Saint-Malo, France in August 1944, and then going back to tell the history of the two protagonists starting in 1934.

Marie-Laure is a young girl who lives with her father in Paris. Her father is a locksmith for the Museum of Natural History. Marie-Laure goes blind at the age of 6 because of cataracts in her eyes. Her father patiently helps her deal with her blindness by giving her Jules Verne novels in braille and by creating a wooden replica of their neighborhood so that she can learn to navigate their neighborhood in Paris despite her blindness.

The second main character, Werner Pfennig, grows up in Zollverein, Germany with his sister, Jutta. They live in an orphanage that is run by a French nun, Frau Elena. Werner is very intelligent, curious, and gifted when it comes to science and engineering. He finds a broken radio and manages to fix it; he and his sister use it to listen to radio broadcasts about science. Werner dreams of becoming a scientist, but due to his social class as a poor orphan, he will be required to work in a coal mine as soon as he turns 15. He gets a chance to escape this fate when he fixes a radio for a Nazi official and is offered a position at a Nazi school in Saxony, Schulpforta.

The rumors of the approaching German occupation grow and the museum prepares for an invasion, making 3 replicas of a priceless diamond named the Sea of Flames. The Sea of Flames is rumored to have a curse surrounding it: the one who keeps it will live forever, but all those he loves will suffer. After the bombing of Paris, Marie-Laure and her father flee the city, her father carrying the Sea of Flames, or a replica—Daniel LeBlanc does not know whether he carries the real or a fake. When her father discovers that the man to whom they were supposed to deliver the diamond has fled the country to go to London, they decide to continue to the house of her great-uncle Etienne in Saint-Malo. Her father once again builds her a model of the city and hides the diamond inside the replica of their house, unbeknownst to anyone, including Marie-Laure. The Germans confiscate all of the radios in Saint-Malo, but Etienne manages to keep one hidden in his attic. Marie-Laure's father is asked to return to the museum but is arrested en route and is placed in a prison camp in Germany.

A Sergeant Major named Reinhardt von Rumpel is given the task of finding and cataloging cultural artifacts wanted by Hitler; the Sea of Flames is the object von Rumpel most wants to find. He at first just wants it for its value to the Reich, but later wants it for personal reasons: to save him from his fate of dying of cancer.

Werner struggles in the environment at Schulpforta, where is only friend is a kind gentle boy named Frederick. Frederick is eventually singled out for punishment because he refused to participate in killing a prisoner. He is badly beaten and nearly dies. He is sent home because his brain has received permanent damage. Werner's skills in math and science are noticed by a teacher, Dr. Hauptmann, who then trains Werner to design a system that can help him locate radio broadcasts. Werner is watched over by an older student, Volkheimer, who is known for his large, intimidating stature and rumored toughness.

Madame Manec, Etienne's housekeeper, organizes a group of women who fought for the resistance against the Nazis. She attempts to get Etienne onboard, but he feels that it is too dangerous. However, after Madame Manec's death, Etienne and Marie-Laure feel compelled to continue her efforts of resistance. Their method involves Marie-Laure going to a bakery in town where she gets loaves of bread from Madame Ruelle that have slips of paper with resistance intelligence baked on the inside. The information is then delivered to Etienne, who broadcasts them on his radio. Near the climax of the novel, Etienne is arrested when he attempts to discover the locations of Nazi anti-aircraft guns to broadcast.

As the war continues, Werner is told he is 18 instead of 16, a lie perpetrated by Dr. Hauptmann so that that Werner can be sent into the military. He joins a special team, with Volkheimer, that hunts down anti-German radio broadcasts and kills the broadcasters. As the novel approaches the climax of the bombing of Saint-Malo, the team moves to Saint-Malo to try and locate another illegal broadcast. Werner realizes that the broadcast in Saint-Malo seems very similar to the science broadcasts he listened to in his youth. Werner doesn't tell his team about the broadcast. He locates it himself, finding Marie-Laure and falling in love with her.

The Allies bomb Saint-Malo. Werner takes shelter in a hotel cellar with Volkheimer and an engineer; the hotel collapses under the bombing, which traps Werner and the two others. Marie-Laure hides in Etienne's cellar until the bombing is over. She goes to the third floor to find water, but ends up hiding in the attic while a Sergeant Major von Rumpel enters her home in a desperate search for the Sea of Flames.

After spending days in the attic, Marie-Laure begins broadcasting on her uncle's radio. Werner, trapped, manages to fix his own radio, and he and Volkheimer hear her reading. While reading she pauses and says that 'He is here'. Werner understands that she is in danger. Instead of waiting to be discovered, Marie-Laure starts to play loud music. Volkheimer hears the music through his radio and decides to start blasting through the rubble where he and Werner are trapped. Werner manages to get out, and rescues Marie-Laure by killing von Rumpel. He helps her escape the city, but before leaving Marie-Laure put the Sea of Flames and the model of the house in an ocean grotto and gives Werner the key. Marie-Laure reunites with Etienne, and the Allies take Werner prisoner. He becomes ill, deliriously wanders into a minefield, and is killed by an explosion.

In 1945, Werner's sister Jutta is in Berlin, working in a factory with Frau Elena and some other girls, when the Russian soldiers arrive and rape her. Marie-Laure and Etienne move to Paris and search for her father, whom they never find.

Years later, Werner's belongings are given to Volkheimer, who gives them to Jutta. One of the items was the model of Etienne's house. Jutta goes to Saint-Malo to find more information about her brother's final days. She realizes that there is a house that matches the model. Someone puts her in touch with Marie-Laure, who now works at the Museum of Natural History. Jutta and Marie-Laure meet. Jutta tells her that Werner died, and gives her the model house. Inside Marie-Laure finds the key to the gate that protects the grotto. She wonders what Werner did with the Sea of Flames. The narrator reveals that Werner left the diamond in the grotto.

The last chapter tells a short narrative of Marie-Laure in 2014, with her grandson, wondering if souls of the dead travel the same airwaves as the cellphone signals and long ago radio signals, and thus are always with us.

All the Light We Cannot See Characters

Marie-Laure LeBlanc

Introduced in Part 0 at age 16, the novel goes back to tell her story from age 6, when she first went completely blind. Marie-Laure is a pretty girl with freckles and auburn hair, who lives with her father in Paris until they are forced to flee during the German invasion, moving to Saint-Malo with her great uncle Etienne. Marie-Laure is bold, curious, imaginative, and highly observational of the sensory details around her, partly due to the fact that she cannot see.

Werner Pfennig

First introduced in Part 0 at age 18, he is a private in the German army in World War II, later telling his story starting from the age of 7, when he is living at an orphanage inside a coal-mining town in Zollverein, Germany. He has a peculiar look: he has white hair, he is always small for his age, and his ears stick out. As the book travels between his childhood and the time period of the bombing of Saint-Malo, Werner is characterized as a markedly intelligent boy in the areas of engineering, science, and math. He struggles between meeting the expectations of the forces around him, especially the ideology of Nazi Germany, and his own feelings of what is right.

Jutta Pfennig

Jutta is first introduced at age 5. She is the younger sister of Werner. She is fascinated by the radio and admires her brother. However, when he decides to go to Schulpforta, a school designed by the Reich to train boys for their army, she is extremely opposed. She does not agree with the actions Germany is taking against other countries, nor with those it's taking against Jews. She is portrayed as a girl with a strong sense of what's right. Later, as an adult she is portrayed as a woman who has tried to forget the trauma of the war, and who feels guilty for what her country has done.

Daniel LeBlanc / Monsieur LeBlanc

Marie-Laure's father. A locksmith at the national museum in Paris. He is the sole caretaker of Marie-Laure. When she goes blind he builds scale models of the places they live so she can study them to understand how to get around her neighborhood.

He also builds puzzle boxes for Marie-Laure, as well as special puzzle-like safes for the museum. He encourages Marie-Laure to use her imagination and sense of adventure through reading and exploring the museum where he works. His relationship with Marie-Laure is very close and loving; he is characterized as patient, sometimes aloof, and forever devoted to Marie-Laure.

Etienne LeBlanc

The great uncle of Marie-Laure, who lives in Saint-Malo. He was in The Great War (World War I) and was traumatized by the death of his brother—Marie-Laure's grandfather, Henri. Etienne is withdrawn and reclusive, and he has a great love of radios, science, and books, which he shares with Marie-Laure. He sometimes sees visions of ghosts or people who are not there, which causes him to panic and stay locked in his room. "Her great-uncle seems kind, curious, and entirely sane. Stillness: this is what he radiates more than anything else. The stillness of a tree. Of a mouse blinking in the dark" (Ch 44).

Frank Volkheimer

An older cadet with Werner at school, he is known as The Giant because of his large stature. Later he is a staff sergeant in the German army with Werner during the bombing of Saint-Malo. Although Volkheimer is rumored to be strong and cruel, and is later shown fulfilling his duty of killing resistance fighters without pause, he also has a soft-spot for Werner, whom he treats almost like a brother. In addition, he loves classical music.

Walter Bernd

An engineer in the army with Werner. He is described as pungent, with misaligned pupils. He hides in the cellar with Werner during the bombing of Saint-Malo. He and Neumann Two often make raunchy commentary.

Frau Elena

The directress of the Children's House where Werner grew up. She is from the Alsace region in France; she is a Protestant nun, and teaches the children French. She likes to drink sherry, and later takes up smoking during the war years. She is characterized as kind, motherly, and not very strict with supervision.

Dr. Geffard

A mollusk expert (malacologist) who works at the National Museum of Natural History in Paris with Marie-Laure's father. He is a kind older man, with a beard, who likes to eat a roasted duck every day at 3 pm. He calls Marie-Laure 'Laurette', and teaches her about mollusks—and more specifically about snails, also known as whelks.

Hans Schilzer and Herribert Pomsel

The two older boys from Children's house who join the Hitler Youth and begin acting superior to the other children in the house.

Claudia Förster

Also known as Big Claudia and described as cow-like, she and Jutta work together on tasks at Children's House. Later, she is one of the last children left at the orphanage, and goes with the others to Berlin to work, where she stops talking completely.

Hannah and Susanne Gerlitz

Twins who live at Children's House; Jutta sometimes helps care for them. Later they are some of the last children left at the house, and go to Berlin to work in a machine parts factory.

Rudolf Seidler and Frau Seidler

A German official who lives in the largest, most elegant house in the town of Zollverein. Frau Siedler, his wife, seems to Werner to be a magical creature, as he has never met a woman like her: she has painted fingernails and smooth white calves.

The führer / Hitler

Historical figure, chancellor of Germany from 1933-1946, leader of the movement of the Third Reich. Referenced frequently in the book as the führer, his presence looms especially in Werner's and von Rumpel's narratives.

Monsieur François Giannot

A friend of the museum who lives outside of Paris in Evreux, where Monsieur LeBlanc and Marie-Laure are supposed to take refuge after fleeing Paris with the Sea of Flames.

Frederick

In Schulpforta, he has the bunk above Werner; they become close friends, with Werner often taking care of him and watching out for him. Described as a reedy boy, thin as a blade of grass, skin as pale as cream. He came to Schulpforta from Berlin; his father is assistant to an ambassador. He is an expert in identifying birds. He secretly wears glasses.

Henri LeBlanc

Marie-Laure's grandfather who died in the Great War/World War I. His room is impeccably maintained by Etienne in their childhood home. Recordings of his voice still exist, and Etienne at one point played them nightly on the radio, followed by a recorded song Henri played on the piano; this recording was "The Professor," to which Jutta and Werner listened as children.

Sergeant Major Reinhold von Rumpel

A German officer who has been given the task of locating and cataloguing objects of cultural value for the führer. He is 41 years old when he is first introduced in June 1940. He has a wife and two daughters. His oldest daughter is named Veronika. In the course of the novel he is diagnosed with cancer. He is characterized as patient, detail-oriented, and cruel.

Dr. Hauptmann

The professor of technical sciences at Schulpforta; he identifies Werner's talent for science and math, and takes him on as a lab assistant. Dr. Hauptmann has two greyhound dogs, and his lab is a fire-lit library. He is mysterious to Werner, who is unsure of what Dr. Hauptmann's connections are and why he has Werner working on all of these mathematical equations. Werner suspects Hauptmann of being cruel and uncaring.

Professor Hublin and the assistant director

Professor Hublin is mineralogist at the National Museum of Natural History in Paris, who gives a tour, along with the assistant director of the museum, to Sergeant Major von Rumpel when he comes to look for the Sea of Flames.

Claude Levitte / Big Claude

The man who runs the Parfumerie in Saint-Malo. He collaborates with the Germans in order to get more rations for himself and his family. He is known as Big Claude because he is a fat man: he is described as having a double chin and beady observant eyes.

Bastian / The Commandant

The leader of the field exercises at Schulpforta, he seems capable of incredible cruelty. He wears hobnailed boots and a jacket decorated in war metals; he has a round belly, and a pitted face. He pits the boys against each other to pick out the weakest in the group; he preaches the nationalist propaganda of the Third Reich.

Bäcker and Ernst Somebody

Bäcker is a boy chosen during field exercises by Bastian, who makes Bäcker choose the weakest of the group. Ernst is the boy chosen as the weakest: a slow runner with dark hair.

Helmut Rödel

A small child at Schulpforta in Werner's age group. He from the south of Germany, and keeps his hands balled in fists nearly all his waking hours. He is the first to choose Frederick as the weakest during field exercises.

Reinhard Wöhlmann, Karl Westerholzer, Martin Burkhard, Dieter Ferdinand

Classmates of Werner's at Schulpforta, some of whose fathers are killed in action.

Frau Schwartzenberger

A Jewish woman who lives in Frederick's building in Berlin. Werner thinks of her as a Jewess: she is the only Jewish person he has ever seen. They share an elevator with her; Werner observes her paper bag of wilted greens, and the star sewn into her threadbare clothes.

Fanni

The maid of Frederick's house, a large woman with baggy arms and a downy face, who is kind and loving towards Frederick.

Frederick's mother

A rich cheerful woman who invites and pays for Werner to come home to Berlin with Frederick for the January recess from Schulpforta. Initially she is characterized as a haughty, arrogant, and social woman. Later, she is characterized as lonely and guilty.

Dupont

A half Algerian man in Paris who specializes in making imitation gems; he constructs the three imitation Seas of Flames, commissioned by the National Museum.

Crazy Hubert Bazin

A veteran from the Great War who sleeps in an alcove behind the library. He lost his nose, eye, and ear in the war, and wears a copper mask over half his face. Marie-Laure describes his breath as smelling like crushed insects. Madame Manec brings him food; he tells Marie-Laure stories of the history of Saint Malo, and later gives her a key to an old kennel filled with snails that exists underneath the ramparts. He mysteriously disappears.

Madame Guiboux

Her son repairs the shoes in Saint-Malo.

Madame and Monsieur Hébrard

Madame and her daughter sort the mail of Saint-Malo, including that of the Germans, and they participate in the resistance. Monsieur Hébrard is the book seller of Saint-Malo.

Madame and Monsieur Ruelle

The bakers of Saint-Malo. Madame Ruelle in particular plays a large role in the resistance, and also helps care for Marie-Laure and Etienne by giving them vegetables.

Madame Blanchard

An ancient widow, who participates in the resistance with Madame Manec.

Neumann Two

An underweight corporal who is Werner's first contact in the Wehrmacht, the division of the army he is sent to. He is addicted to pills. He likes to talk about sex.

Neumann One

The 30-year-old driver of the Opel, the truck that Werner's team uses to drive for their duties in the Wehrmacht.

The Viennese girl

Werner first sees her playing outside in the empty city of Vienna, a little redheaded girl in a maroon cape, about six or seven years old, small for her age. She has big clear eyes that remind him of Jutta's. Moments later, in a misled attempt to find a partisan radio broadcast, Neumann Two shoots both the girl and her mother in their own apartment. In the following chapters, the girl haunts Werner, and he frequently sees her hovering above him.

Albert Wette

Jutta's husband in Part 12. A kind, balding accountant, who loves running model trains in their basement.

Max

Jutta's 6-year-old son in Part 12. Curious, clever, asks questions no one and loves making paper airplanes.

John

A Canadian scientist and Marie-Laure's one time lover, who is described as leaving objects scattered around any room he enters. He is the father of Marie-Laure's child, Hélène, in Part 12.

Hélène

Marie-Laure's daughter in Part 12. A short-haired, petite, 19-year old aspiring violinist, described as self-possessed; she lives with Marie-Laure.

Michel

Marie-Laure's 12-year-old grandson in Part 13, who plays online games and patiently walks his grandmother through the Jardin des Plantes.

All the Light We Cannot See Glossary

Agoraphobia

extreme or irrational fear of open or public places.

Asceticism

characterized by abstinence from worldly pleasures, often for the purpose of pursuing spiritual goals.

Artifice

clever or cunning devices or expedients, especially as used to trick or deceive others.

Blazonry

brilliant decoration or display.

Burden

that which is carried; load; that which is borne with difficulty; obligation; onus.

Captor

a person who has captured a person or thing.

Conduit

a pipe that carries water.

Corsair

a swift ship that is often used for piracy.

Deceitful

intended to deceive; misleading; fraudulent: a deceitful action.

Detachment

a group of troops, aircraft, or ships sent away on a separate mission.

Entropy

lack of order or predictability; gradual decline into disorder.

Essen

the city in Germany near which the town of Zollverein is located.

Establishment

something established; a constituted order or system.

Extirpate

to fully destroy something.

Flak

anti-aircraft fire.

Galvanized

to stimulate or excite as if by an electric shock.

Gefreiter

a German, Swiss, and Austrian military rank that has existed since the 16th century. It is usually the second rank or grade to which an enlisted soldier, airman, or sailor could be promoted.

Included / Slightly Included

terms used to qualify diamonds. Because they are formed deep within the earth, under extreme heat and pressure, virtually all diamonds contain "birthmarks": small imperfections inside the diamond called inclusions.

Jules Verne's Around the World in Eighty Days and Twenty Thousand Leagues Under the Sea

Jules Verne was a writer who lived 1828-1905. *Around the World in Eighty Days* was published in 1873; in the story, Phileas Fogg of London and his French valet attempt to circumnavigate the world in 80 days. The other book Marie-Laure reads is the two volume set of *Twenty Thousand Leagues Under the Sea*, originally published in 1870, telling the story of Professor Pierre Aronnax, a French marine biologist and the narrator of the story, Canadian whaler and master harpoonist Ned Land and Aronnax's faithful servant Conseil, who are sent on a mission to find and destroy a sea monster. However, when they find the monster, it is actually the submarine, the Nautilus, of Captain Nemo, who captures them and takes them aboard. From there they go on a series of adventures. ("Jules Verne")

Lapidary

a person who cuts, polishes, or engraves gems.

Loftiness

exalted in rank, dignity, or character; eminent.

Loupe-Clean

diamonds that have no inclusions visible to the naked eye are of excellent quality. The very best—and rarest—clarity is called 'loupe clean'.

Molders

slowly decay or disintegrate, especially because of neglect.

Malouins

people who live in Saint Malo.

Operation Typhoon

the German offensive carried out as part of the Battle of Moscow that occurred between October 1941 and January 1942. ("Battle of Moscow")

Occuper

"to occupy" in French.

Parapet

a low protective wall along the edge of a roof, bridge, or balcony.

Partisan

(in a country that has been defeated) a member of a secret armed force whose aim is to fight against an enemy that is controlling the country.

Passion

any powerful or compelling emotion or feeling, like love or hate.

Phrenology

the study of the conformation of the skull based on the belief that it is indicative of mental faculties and character.

preternaturally

very unusual in a way that does not seem natural.

Prussia

a kingdom that contained parts of Germany, and dissolved in 1914. The Kingdom of Prussia is now divided among the countries of Germany, Poland, and Switzerland, among others. The region of Prussia in Germany is where Volkheimer grew up.

Ruhr

a river in Germany.

Raciological

the study of race as a scholarly discipline, the study sometimes called "racial anthropology" or "scientific racism."

Ramparts

a defensive wall of a castle or walled city, having a broad top with a walkway and typically a stone parapet.

Remnant

a fragment or scrap.

Schulpforta

the National Political Institute of Education at Schulpforta. These institutes were founded to educate next generation of elite leaders in Germany, both political or military, to continue the work started by Hitler. (Trueman)

Stentorian

a loud and powerful sound, often used to describe voices.

Sublimity

when something is sublime, it transcends greatness or beauty for the observer — like a deeply moving film or a transcendent piece of music. So when something is truly wonderful, or someone acts in a truly noble way, it's an example of sublimity.

Sycophantic

(of a person or of behavior) praising people of authority in a way that is not sincere, usually in order to get some advantage from them.

Walloon

people from Wallonia, the French-speaking region of southern Belgium.

Untermensch (german)

a person considered racially or socially inferior.

Vicious

addicted to or characterized by vice; grossly immoral; depraved.

Wehrmacht

the unified armed forces of Nazi Germany from 1935 to 1946.

Zephyr

a soft gentle breeze.

All the Light We Cannot See Themes

Nationalism

Nationalism comes out in two distinct ways in the novel: the nationalistic propaganda of the Nazis, and the nationalism of the resistance fighters in France. In Nazi Germany, this nationalism focused on purity, a group mentality of the goodness of the country, and the acceptability of cruelty as a way of meeting these goals. In France, the theme focuses more on those in Saint-Malo who are not willing to lie down under unwanted Nazi rule, who instead build an unlikely team of resistance including older women, the blind character Marie-Laure, and characters such as Etienne and Crazy Hubert Bazin, both framed as “crazy." Despite the limitations of these unlikely resistance members, together they are able to carry the power in their hands to fight for the freedom of their country.

Science and Technology

The science and technology of radio is specifically relevant to the novel, from Werner’s initial love of the radio show he hears, to his later talent for fixing and engineering radios that are used to further the Nazi propaganda. Etienne and Marie-Laure have a parallel love for radio and the magic of it going into the airwaves; they also use it as a nationalist French tool, both to further the resistance and to connect French people to each other in a time of need.

In addition, the scientific topics of the radio show Werner listened to as a child, which were written by Etienne, emphasize the importance of science in the novel: the science of discovery and learning. Marie-Laure experiences this as well in her exploration of the Natural History Museum, her informal lessons on mollusks with Dr. Geffard, and the reading and adventures she does with Etienne through authors such as Darwin and Jules Verne.

Science provides access to new worlds—both literally, in the sense that Werner escaped his fate in the coal mines by honing his skills in engineering, and figuratively, in the escape that Etienne and Marie-Laure seek from the German-occupied city they live in.

Imagination

The fairy tale nature of the story is played out in some of the characters' other-worldliness: Werner and Jutta as snowy-haired orphans in a soot-covered mine,

Volkheimer as ogre, and Marie-Laure as blind but with the power to see more than many of those around her (Smith). This type of imagery brings a piece of the supernatural into the real and bleak setting of World War II in the novel. In addition, imagination allows the characters of the novel to escape their daily reality, aiding them in surviving: Jutta and Werner play in the trash, collecting objects, creating toys; Daniel LeBlanc finds satisfaction in creating intricate puzzles for his daughter to solve; and Marie-Laure and Etienne imagine journeys to other worlds.

Memory

Memory and the feelings that accompany it are a strong driving force of the actions in the book: they are the way Werner makes it through his schooling, calling up images of childhood to avoid focusing on torture; they are how Marie-Laure is able to solve the puzzle of where the Sea of Flames is located, by remembering her father's cryptic words; they are what motivates von Rumpel to be patient as he carries out his tasks. Often memories come to the characters and are highlighted to the reader in italics. This creates a sort of repetitious song throughout the novel, as phrases the characters heard, on the radio, from loved ones, or things they read, such as Jules Verne, or science texts, continually appear. As the context changes, the meaning of the phrase often changes as well. Thus memory in the novel is used to emphasize, throughout the chapters, the relationships between a character and his or her experiences, and the people he or she has met along the way, and how these have shaped him or her. In addition, characters also often fall back into complete reveries of childhood, or time spent with loved ones. For example, Werner uses his more pleasant memories to avoid his current reality, but as his life and his guilt grow more complicated, his good memories soon all begin to blend together, and he is haunted by the memories of the terrible things he has been a part of.

Familial loyalty and love

One review describes this as "a novel that celebrates the power of family and love." Marie-Laure's great-uncle Etienne says "If your same blood doesn't run in the arms and legs of the person you're next to, you can't trust anything" (ch 84), because he believes that during these hard times, the only people who can be trusted are family. However, the novel also places value on the family one constructs around oneself: the relationship between Etienne and Madame Manec, the relationship between Werner and Volkheimer, and between Frau Elena with Werner and Jutta—people who share no blood yet have devotion, love, and loyalty between them. It is this bond that helps the characters to survive some of the major conflicts of the novel.

Darkness and light

The novel constantly employs imagery of literal darkness and light, especially through the motif of vision and sight. Aside from literally seeing or not seeing, this theme exploring a deeper meaning of lightness and darkness: that of good and evil, and of the places where they overlap. Werner, with his hair as white as snow, is a character whose actions are less than pure, as he is pulled deeper and deeper into the war. Marie-Laure, who is in the "dark" of her own blindness, actually encompasses more of the good of the novel, seeing through to the kindness and goodness in people, and sensing the dark sides of the people who are trying to harm her or her family. Can the darkness and the light, the evil and the good, exist simultaneously inside these characters, in their actions, and in their lives?

Humanism and fate/destiny

Anthony Doerr intentionally wrote a novel that questions and celebrates human will and choice (Tweed). The philosophy of Humanism asserts that humanity must take responsibility for its own destiny ("Definition of Humanism"). The children of the novel are stuck in a war in which they must make decisions: Werner must choose whether to follow the ideology of the nationalism around him, and Marie-Laure must choose whether to participate in the resistance actively in a way that may endanger others, at one point asking, "But we are the good guys. Aren't we, Uncle?" (Ch 116.) In addition, while the Sea of Flames allegory may seem to indicate a sort of planned destiny—living forever among the suffering of others—there is also a choice in the matter: the stone could simply be tossed into the sea, absolving the curse.

All the Light We Cannot See Quotes and Analysis

"A corner of the night sky, beyond a wall of trees, blooms red. In the lurid, flickering light, he sees that the airplane was not alone, that the sky teems with them, a dozen swooping back and forth, racing in all directions, and in a moment of disorientation, he feels that he's looking not up but down, as though a spotlight has been shined into a wedge of bloodshot water, and the sky has become the sea, and the airplanes are hungry fish, harrying their prey in the dark."

(Ch 17) Daniel LeBlanc

As the war arrives in France and Daniel and Marie-Laure LeBlanc flee Paris, Daniel awakes in the night to see this nightmarish image of his city being bombed. It seems to unreal to him that he momentarily sees it as an inverted image. This plays on the motif of light and darkness: the light here is "lurid, flickering," and "bloodshot," all indicating its evil nature.

"Werner was back in Zollverein, standing above a grave a miner had dug for two mules at the edge of a field, and it was winter and Werner was no older than five, and the skin of the mules had grown nearly translucent, so that their bones were hazily visible inside, and little clods of dirt were stuck to their open eyes, and he was hungry enough to wonder if there was anything left on them worth eating.He heard the blade of a shovel strike pebbles. He heard his sister inhale."

(Ch 34) Werner

This image occurs to Werner as he is being buried by the debris in the cellar from the bombing of Saint-Malo. The story of the dead mule is an allegory for his own fear of dying, starved, alone, eyes open but unseeing in the darkness; the image is visceral and almost nauseating in the way the clods of dirt are stuck to the mule's eyes and the way he hears in the memory the sounds of the shovel and his sister breathing. It reflects on the current moment, where Werner is being buried similarly, while still alive.

"Her Majesty, the Austrians call their cannon, and for the past week these men have tended to it the way worker bees might tend to a queen. They've fed her oils, repainted her barrel, lubricated her wheels; they've arranged sandbags at her feet like offerings."

(Ch 4) Werner

The simile endows the cannon with the power that a Queen Bee has over her workers: all the work they do is for the purpose of honoring her. The context of the Queen Bee imagery is the hotel where the Austrian Detachment and Werner's small unit have installed themselves. Underneath this simile lurks the theme of nationalism, as the cannon is working as a defense of the country, protecting what the Germans and the Austrians stand for in their devotion to a larger source: their country and its purity under the Reich.

> *"The brain is locked in total darkness, of course, children, says the voice. It floats in a clear liquid inside the skull, never in the light. And yet the world it constructs in the mind is full of light. It brims with color and movement. So how, children, does the brain, which lives without a spark of light, build for us a world full of light?"*
>
> *(Ch 18) Werner and Jutta*

The motif of light and darkness and the theme of science are brought together here in the "Professor's" talk on light and the way the brain works. What he says is a paradox, and yet it is true, which is what draws the attention of both Werner and Jutta. They cannot see the speaker, but he creates imagery for them, not only of how the brain is, but also of how light interacts with it; he creates for Werner and Jutta a magical world of science that they want to explore.

> *When Werner overhears Frederick's mother say to a woman, "Oh, the Schwartzenberger crone will be gone by year's end, then we'll have the top floor, du wirst schon sehen," he glances at Frederick, whose smudged eyeglasses have gone opaque in the candlelight, whose makeup looks strange and lewd now, as though it has intensified the bruises rather than concealed them, and a feeling of great uneasiness overtakes him.*
>
> *(Ch 68) Werner*

Werner's doubts about his role in the war and the Nazis have been present from the very beginning, highlighted most by his sister Jutta's goodness/ethical purity. However, this is the moment where Werner realizes that the choices he is making are no different than the discrimination he sees in Frederick's mother's remarks about Frau Schwartzenberger; the same violence that harmed his friend Frederick, who in this moment appears to Werner with amplified injuries. Even in a scene that initially radiated comfort, luxury, and pride, fitting in with the theme of nationalism and purity, Werner's most humanistic side suddenly realizes that all of those things come on the backs of others who are being harmed.

> *Twist the chimney ninety degrees, slide off the roof panels one two three.*
>
> *A fourth door, and a fifth, on and on until you reach a thirteenth, a little locked door no bigger than a shoe.*
>
> *So, asked the children, how do you know it's really there?*

You have to believe the story.

She turns the little house over. A pear-shaped stone drops into her palm.

(Ch 142) Marie-Laure

Puzzles are a symbol that appear throughout the book, reminding the reader of the light we cannot see: things are not always as they appear. Here, Marie-Laure discovers that the "dumb" model of Saint-Malo that her father left her, was part of an elaborate chamber constructed to hold the valuable diamond, the Sea of Flames. While Marie-Laure solves this puzzle, the theme of memory arises: she uses the memory she has of the first introduction to the Sea of Flames to convince herself of the intricate puzzle constructed around the Sea of Flames—literally in the form of the series of locks, but also figuratively in terms of the curse surrounding the stone.

Frederick said we don't have choices, don't own our lives, but in the end it was Werner who pretended there were no choices, Werner who watched Frederick dump the pail of water at his feet—I will not—Werner who stood by as the consequences came raining down. Werner who watched Volkheimer wade into house after house, the same ravening nightmare recurring over and over and over.

(Ch 133) Werner

Werner realizes that Frederick embodies the theme of humanism: making decisions for the good of humans, out of kindness, and not out of conditioning towards a cruel goal of purity and nationalism. Werner realizes that he too can choose to act this way himself.

"She crouches over her knees. She is the Whelk. Armored. Impervious."

(Ch 137) Marie-Laure

The whelk in the novel is a symbol closely related to Marie-Laure; here, she embodies the whelk and she is in her "shell" of the grotto under the ramparts, protecting herself from von Rumpel, who waits outside.

The violins spiral down, then back up. Etienne takes Marie-Laure's hand and together, beneath the low, sloping roof—the record spinning, the transmitter sending it over the ramparts, right through the bodies of the Germans and out to sea—they dance.

(Ch 106) Etienne

This quote features the themes of familial love and loyalty, as well as the motif of radio transmission. For Etienne, what has helped make him feel most alive is his relationship with Marie-Laure, as well as his ability to participate in the resistance specifically because of his talent for radio transmission.

To shut your eyes is to guess nothing of blindness. Beneath your world of skies and faces and buildings exists a rawer and older world, a place where surface planes disintegrate and sounds ribbon in shoals through the air.

(Ch 27) Marie-Laure

The motif of vision and sight is an important part of the plot, specifically in the irony that Marie-Laure has the ability to "see" more than other sighted people This passage leads into an elegant series of images of things Marie-Laure can hear and feel both near and far away; she in fact, is able to "see" all the light we cannot. She sees the beauty, the quietness, and the humanity that others often miss.

All the Light We Cannot See Epigraph & Chapters 1 - 31 (Part 0: 7 August 1944 & Part 1: 1934) Summary and Analysis

Summary

Epigraph

A quote from Philip Beck recounts the fact that the city of Saint-Malo, on the Coast of Brittany, France, was bombed in August 1944. Another quote from Joseph Goebbels states that the Nazis would not have been able to take power without the radio.

Part 0: 7 August 1944

1: Leaflets

Leaflets that say "Urgent message to the inhabitants of this town. Depart immediately to open country" fall from the sky on a small city in France, Saint-Malo. American bombers are coming and have begun to drop bombs.

2: Bombers

The perspective switches to the American bombardiers, who fly over the English channel towards the coastal cities they will bomb.

3: The Girl

Marie-Laure LeBlanc, age 16, is inside a house in Saint-Malo. She is blind. She is kneeling in front of and touching a scale model of the city she is in. There are buckets filled with water in the corner of the room, in case the water goes out again. She finds one of the leaflets in her window and smells its fresh ink. She can hear the airplanes coming.

4: The Boy

Werner Pfennig, an 18-year-old German Private, is 5 blocks north of Marie-Laure, in a building that was once a hotel, L'hôtel des Abeilles, or the Hotel of Bees. The building was once owned by a wealthy privateer with a fascination with bees, hence the bee murals in the building. Later the home became an elegant hotel, but over the past 4 weeks it has been transformed into a fortress. Werner is told to go into the basement. Above him, a detachment of Austrians prepare to fire off their cannon, a "high-velocity anti-air gun called an 88" against the American bombardiers. They care for the cannon as if it were a queen bee. As they fire the cannon they sing. Werner enters the cellar.

5: Saint-Malo

The people remaining in the city are prostitutes, nuns, drunks, the blind, and others who have been slow to leave. This town is the last German strongpoint on the Breton coast, even if it seems they are losing the war elsewhere. Rumors say that the Germans have built underground corridors, have stores of ammunition, and the like. Saint-Malo is a city surrounded by water on 4 sides. Anti-air batteries fire from the outer islands. Frenchmen imprisoned on an island called Fort National huddle and look up.

6: Number 4 rue Vauborel

Marie-Laure does not go into the cellar to hide. She instead goes to the scale model and selects the house she lives in, the house of her great-uncle Etienne. She releases a hidden catch and lifts the house up. In a series of motions she unlocks a chamber inside the house and releases a stone into her palm.

7: Cellar

Werner sits in the cellar of the Hotel of Bees and connects himself to a radio, wearing headphones. From this radio he can communicate with a transceiver upstairs in the hotel, as well as with two other anti-air batteries outside of Saint-Malo. Sergeant Frank Volkheimer and an engineer named Bernd join Werner in the cellar. Werner realizes he forgot water. The Austrians continue firing the gun 4 floors above. Werner thinks of his childhood, with his sister Jutta, and Frau Elena tying his shoes.

8: Bombs Away

The bombs drop, 480 bombs altogether, and the sky is filled with black specks. Marie-Laure's great uncle, locked with others in Fort National off the shore, thinks of the locusts, a plague from the Old Testament. In the city, it is an avalanche, a hurricane, everything inaudible. The anti-air guns fire their last shells, the bombers leave the city themselves unharmed. Marie-Laure crawls under her bed holding the miniature house in one hand and the stone in the other. In the cellar where Werner is, the light bulb goes out.

Part 1: 1934

9: Muséum National d'Histoire Naturelle

Marie-Laure is a 6-year-old in Paris with deteriorating eyesight. She is taking a tour of the museum her father works at. At the end of the tour, they arrive at a set of doors that no one is allowed to enter. The guide tells the children the story of a stone called the Sea of Flames. In the story, a prince in Borneo finds the stone in a dry riverbed, but on his way home he is robbed and stabbed. However, the stone remains clutched in his hand, and he manages to crawl home. There, he miraculously recovers. They begin to think the stone has healing powers. Jewelers say the stone is a large raw diamond, and they have it faceted, revealing its brilliant blue color with a touch of red at the center; thus it came to be known as the Sea of Flames. However, as the prince kept the stone, his loved ones began to die, and an army began to gather to attack him. One priest tells the prince of a dream he had, where the Goddess of the Earth told him she'd made the Sea of Flames for the God of the Sea, and was sending him the jewel through the river. But when the prince took the jewel from the dry river bed, the Goddess became angry and cursed the stone. The curse was that the keeper of the stone would live forever, but those he loved would be unlucky. Still, the prince decides to keep the stone. After his city is raided and all are killed, he disappears, and the stone does not reappear again for 200 years, at which point it appears in India. A Duke in Europe buys the gem, and his family members and servants begin to die or become ill. The duke thus has the stone locked in the vaults of the museum in Paris, with special instructions not to open the vaults for 200 years. Four more years remain before the vault can be opened. Marie-Laure asks why the stone can't be thrown into the sea, and everyone laughs because the value of the stone is so high that no one would ever want to do that.

10: Zollverein

Werner Pfennig is from a German town called Zollverein, a coal mining town 300 miles north of Paris. He and his sister live in an Orphanage called Children's House. The economy of Germany at the time makes rations scarce, and there is often little to eat. At seven years old, he has a way about him that seems to charm people; his hair is a milky white color. He is creative and curious, constantly asking Frau Elena questions about how things work. Frau Elena is a Protestant nun from Alsace (France), who tells the children stories in French about her hometown, and sings them lullabies in French as well.

Werner and his sister Jutta draw together, and Jutta has a talent for drawing. They also venture together to sift through garbage and find treasures or useful items. Sometimes they go to look down into the largest mine, Pit Nine, where their father died.

11: Key Pound

Marie-Laure is diagnosed with Bilateral Cataracts: she will never see again. She struggles to make her way through her own house; nothing makes sense to her. People pity her and her father. Her mother died in childbirth. She only feels safe in her bed, where her father sits next to her and carves his scale models.

After the despair passes, they begin a ritual where Marie-Laure and her father wake up together, drink coffee with lots of sugar, and then go to the museum where her father works. Her father is the museum locksmith, in charge of the key pound inside the museum, where thousands of keys are kept—handed out by him, and returned to him daily. Her father tests Marie-Laure's memory by having her identify types of keys, and by placing random objects in her hands. He also has her begin to practice braille. Dr. Geffard, a mollusk expert, sometimes watches Marie-Laure and teaches her about different seashells, calling her Laurette. He likes to eat a roasted duck for lunch. Marie-Laure discovers her sense of touch through the objects in the museum. In the evenings they eat dinner, her father telling her where the food is on the plate by using the hands of a clock, and after supper her father works on his scale model of the neighborhood. Mondays are their day off.

12: Radio

Werner finds a radio when he is eight years old. It looks just like a spool of metal with electrical leads and an earphone. When he gets it home it doesn't work, but after three weeks Werner figures out a way to rewire it so it does work. Finally, he is able to hear sound, a symphony of music. He passes the earphone to Jutta so she can listen too.

13: Take Us Home

Every birthday, Marie-Laure receives a gift from her father, a puzzle box that she has to solve to discover some item inside. When she turns 7, a puzzle box waits on the table where the sugar bowl usually is. After a series of tricks, she opens it and finds chocolate inside.

The model neighborhood that her father is making still does not make sense to her: she cannot match it to the reality outside their door. Marie-Laure's perception of the neighborhood is filled with sounds and smells; the model is quiet and smells like sawdust. However, one day about a year after Marie-Laure has gone completely blind, her father takes her to a familiar path and asks her to lead them home, based on the model. She uses a cane to find her way around. However, Marie-Laure is not able to succeed at this task. Her father has faith that she can and will learn how to get back home.

14: Something Rising

Werner has become an expert at improving his radio. He gathers materials from supply sheds, and convinces local shopkeepers to give him unneeded items. Every evening he brings the radio downstairs so the other children can listen for an hour. All have different shows they like, including Frau Elena. Werner notes that mine production has increased and unemployment has dropped; better food begins to come to their orphanage, and they receive new Bibles, new clothes, and shoes.

In the fall of 1936, the children listen to a state-sponsored radio play about invaders sneaking into a village at night, plotting to murder children. The invaders are discovered, a patriotic march plays, and all are happy again.

15: Light

Marie-Laure continues to try to lead her father home every Tuesday, but she does not succeed until she is eight years old. She studies the miniature of their neighborhood to count the number of benches and storm drains. When she is leading him home she counts buildings, trees, intersections, and the sounds she hears of branches. It is snowing on the day she leads them both home correctly the first time. When they arrive her father lifts her up and laughs, and they turn in circles together.

16: Our Flag Flutters Before Us

Two older boys at Children's House, Hans Schilzer and Herribert Pomsel, join the Hitler Youth. They begin to carry slingshots and bully younger children. They sit in the town square and say, "'Good evening… or *Heil* Hitler if you prefer." They chant sayings about their flag, brag about their rifle training, and tease anyone who admires something foreign in a book. Frau Elena does not speak French around them, and watches them warily. Werner tries to avoid them, instead focusing his attention on popular science magazines. An official from the Labor Ministry comes to speak about work at the mines, which all boys will have to do starting at age 15. Werner thinks of his father who died in the mine, his body never recovered. The official from the Labor Ministry talks about coal as the fuel, and thus the foundation, of the nation.

17: Around the World in Eighty Days

Marie-Laure has begun to measure the things around her in the number of paces, drawing maps in her head. She explores by following hedges, cables, and pipes. She can identify the different smells of the different departments of the museum. Children she meets asks her questions about how it feels to be blind. Although she never knows if the lights are on, she doesn't experience her blindness as darkness. In fact, she sees colors in her imagination and in her dreams. Different sounds and objects are associated with color for Marie-Laure. She gets lost inside the museum at times, exploring.

When she turns nine her father leaves a new puzzle on the table, as usual, and gives her a braille copy of Jules Verne's *Around the World in 80 Days*. She begins to read it and the braille becomes easier for her. She reads it twice through.

18: The Professor

Jutta and Werner find copper wire and bring it home to use on their radio. They think they hear someone talking in Russian. They stay up late listening to the radio. They hear a Professor speaking in French about the brain, and how it is locked in darkness but constructs a world full of light in the mind. He talks about how the coal in the furnace used to be a plant millions of years ago. Werner is fascinated because the man is talking about exactly the types of things that he is curious about. The broadcast ends in piano music.

19: Sea of Flames

Rumors circulate through the Paris museum about the Sea of Flames, what it looks like, where it came from, and whether the legend behind it is real. Everyone has a slightly different story of what it looks like and what the curse will do to a person. Marie-Laure knows it has been 4 years since she was told the story of the Sea of Flames on her tour of the museum. Marie-Laure asks her father if he believes in the curse. He says the tales of the curse are just stories. However, whenever anything goes wrong at the museum, the staff blames the diamond. Monsieur LeBlanc is called to build a special case to display the diamond, and Marie-Laure is never allowed to accompany him on his work. Marie-Laure spends time with Dr. Geffard, who tells her how diamonds and crystals grow over many years, and how the rock may have a long history of being worn by queens or pharaohs. Marie-Laure's concern is that her father has not been anywhere near the diamond.

20: Open Your Eyes

Werner and Jutta continue to find the French broadcasts and listen to them. The Professor talks about how the brain works, the nature of light, sea creatures, and the North Pole. He gives experiments that Jutta and Werner repeat on their own. They want to know where he broadcasts from. Werner feels that the quality of the broadcasts degrades week by week. At night, while Jutta is asleep beside him, Werner fantasizes that he is an engineer in a laboratory looking through a telescope.

21: Fade

Marie-Laure's father's work on the special project comes to a close, he becomes available again to her to go on walks and errands. Nothing new happens at the museum. When Marie-Laure turns 11, she receives a puzzle: a wooden cube that takes 13 steps to open, with two bonbons inside. She also receives a new book, *Twenty Thousand Leagues Under the Sea*—the first part. The narrator in the book works at the same museum her father works at. She spends time with her book, seeing distant places described there.

22: The Principles of Mechanics

A vice minister and his wife visit Children's House. All the children are on their best behavior. The minister and his wife eat dinner with the children. Werner sits with a book in his lap, *The Principles of Mechanics*. He is absorbed in reading, and at one point he looks up to find everyone staring at him. The vice minister asks if it is a "jew book" and confiscates it. Jutta tells everyone that her brother is good at mathematics and he will go to study with great scientists in Berlin. The vice minister says that the only place Werner will be going is into the mines. Everyone is completely silent for the rest of dinner.

23: Rumors

Rumors circulate that the Germans are coming, that they can march for four days straight, that they impregnate every schoolgirl they see, and other horrible tales. Monsieur LeBlanc tells Marie-Laure that the director of the museum is not worried about this, so she should not be either. Nothing seems to change. She continues to read *Twenty Thousand Leagues Under the Sea*. Dr. Geffard teacher her the names of shells and explains marine evolution. He also explains that almost all species that has ever lived has gone extinct, meaning humans may someday do the same. The smells of summer remain the same as usual to Marie-Laure, but in early autumn she feels she can smell gasoline underneath the wind, as if a huge machine were coming towards her.

24: Bigger Faster Brighter

Werner is required to join the State Youth because membership is mandatory; the boys are quizzed on fitness standards and nationalism about the glory of the country. Werner continues listening to the radio, going over the equations he copied from his mechanics book that was confiscated. He likes to repair things, such as sewing machines, and invent machines that can do things such as slicing a whole carrot at once. He begins to repair the radios of neighbors, and becomes popular among them. They pay him in marks (currency) or in food. One day Jutta tells Werner that a girl she knows was kicked out of a swimming hole for being a half-breed—i.e. a half-Jew. One of two boys who joined Hitler youth, Herribert Pomsel, now is 15 and working at the mines; the other, Hans Schlizer, is an unruly teenager who fights with Frau Elena.

25: Mark of the Beast

In November 1939 Marie-Laure is reading *Twenty Thousand Leagues Under the Sea* in a park, when some boys come up to her and says, "They're mad for blind girls, you know." Her cane rolls off the bench, and even after they are called away by an adult, she is panicked. The stores are selling gas masks. She asks her father what will happen to them if there is a war. He tells her all will be fine, but she can hear him reading the news urgently. She has nightmares of Germans.

At the end of the chapter, before the next chapter begins, an italicized letter from Jutta appears. The letter is written to the "Professor" and states that they have not heard him in two months, and are worried that the Deutschland broadcasts are pushing out every other broadcast. She reports she has to come straight home from school now, even though she is not a Jew. Also, listening to foreign channels is a criminal offense. She also says that her brother will not help her send the letter, so she is going to send it herself.

26: Good Evening. Or *Heil* Hitler if You Prefer.

May 1940, Werner turns 14, the Children's House celebrates, they listen to the radio. In one more year Werner will have to go to work in the mines. He hasn't heard the Frenchman Professor on the radio in months. He hasn't had his *Principles of Mechanics* book for a year. He has nightmares of being inside the mine, the ceiling crushing him. Outside it is raining; he looks out and thinks of it as the ever-expanding machine of Germany.

27: Bye-Bye, Blind Girl

The war is going to happen, and Monsieur LeBlanc works hard at the museum to prepare, safeguarding the precious items there. Marie-Laure observes spring continuing as usual. She turns 12, and although her father has been too busy to make her a puzzle, she receives the second volume of *Twenty Thousand Leagues Under the Sea*. People in the apartments around them are packing up their things. Marie-Laure goes to the museum with her father and tries to read, but she is distracted. In June, airplanes fly over the city, and they begin to lose radio signal. Marie-Laure feels she can sense a shiver in the air. She had thought everything was always going to be the same, but now what?

28: Making Socks

Werner wakes in the night and sees Jutta listening to the radio. She wants to know why she has to make so many socks in Young Girls League. Werner wants to know what Jutta is listening to; she tells him the radio is saying they are dropping bombs on Paris.

29: Flight

In Paris people pack up and hide their valuables. At the museum Monsieur LeBlanc is called to the director's office; Marie-Laure tries to read, but is distracted by all the preparation. The museum is packed up and emptied. Marie-Laure hopes that this is all a puzzle, a game her father constructed. Distinct thumps begin to happen outside. Her father comes to get her and tells her to leave her book behind. They go back to the apartment and gather items for their flight. Marie-Laure's father tells her to go to the bathroom because it may be a while before she can again. They go to an area of the city she has never been before. Her father tells her they have tickets arranged on a train. However, the train station is full of people, all of them hoping for a train.

30: Herr Seidler

A corporal comes to the door of the Children's House and asks for Werner. Frau Elena is very nervous, as is Werner. Werner goes with the man to the house of Herr Seidler. Rudolf Seidler lives in the nicest house in their town, and Werner has never been this close to it before. Inside Werner is surprised by the luxury of the home: the thick carpet, the smell of cake, and the huge elaborate American radio. Werner is introduced to Herr Seidler and asked to fix the radio. Herr Seidler's wife sits nearby the radio reading a magazine. Werner nervously takes a look at the inner workings of the radio and talks to himself, saying "think" out loud. He finds the problem, a simple one, and fixes it. The radio begins to work and Frau Seidler is delighted, commenting that he fixed the radio just by thinking. She comes over to the radio, and Werner observes that she is barefoot and has smooth white calves. Herr Seidler invites Werner to eat cake. Werner is presented with four pieces of cake dusted in powdered sugar with a dollop of cream. Herr Seidler acknowledges that cream is forbidden, but simply says that he has his ways. He also says he likes the posting in the coal town, although there are more desirable places for posts, such as France. He comments that Werner is very smart and should go to a specialized school. Werner responds that he has no money. However, Herr Seidler says he will write a letter to this school, which specifically wants working class boys like Werner. Werner returns to Children's House, and Frau Elena and Jutta anxiously greet him. Frau Elena is relieved that they only wanted Werner to fix the radio, and not for questioning about Children's House. That night Werner destroys his own small coil radio by crushing it with a brick.

31: Exodus

Marie-Laure and her father wait for the train to come for hours, but it never does. They decide to walk. The streets are all filled with cars and with other people walking. Marie-Laure observes the voices of the panicked people around her. They reach the outskirts of Paris. Marie-Laure's heels are bleeding. She and her father go into a half-mowed field of grass near a farm house, which looks as if the farmer had stopped in the middle of his work. They eat some bread and sausage and Marie-Laure asks her father where they are going. They are headed to the house of a man who the museum said will help them, named Monsieur Giannot, in Evreux. While Marie-Laure sleeps her father takes a blue stone out of his tool kit. He has one of 4 stones made to look like the Sea of Flames. 3 stones are fake and one is real. One decoy is at the museum. The other two stones are with other museum workers who also have safe havens in different directions. Monsieur Leblanc wonders if the one he has is real. He wakes in the night to see a plane flying over and then bombing in the distance. He realizes there are many planes above him, and he gets the sensation as if he were looking down rather than up: down into an ocean of hungry fish.

Analysis

The book begins with an epigraph containing two quotes. The first quote tells the reader details about the bombing of Saint-Malo that occurred in 1944, and how it was carried out. This quote sets the scene for Part 0, as well as for the upcoming parts of the book that take place during this bombing, giving historical facts to add setting and background details. In addition, there is a quote from Joseph Goebbels, the Reich Minister of Propaganda of Nazi Germany from 1933 to 1945. Goebbels' quote is an insight into the minds of the politicians running the Third Reich, who were very aware that the dissemination of their propaganda via radio specifically, was essential to the creation of the movement of the Reich, the formation of the Nazis, and the belief and trust in the Nationalist ideology—a theme that is woven throughout the novel, interlaced with the motif of radio transmission.

In Part 0, the narration starts in medias res—in the middle of the action leading toward the climax later on in the book. Doerr specifically chose to start here because of the historical nature of the novel: he knew it should not be a surprise that the bombing of Saint-Malo occurred; what is new about this narrative is the characters and their reaction and survival in this context (Smith). Marie-Laure and Werner, only 5 blocks from each other, prepare for the bombing. In a great use of contrast, Marie-Laure is filling buckets with water, while Werner forgot water; Marie-Laure is on the top floor of her house, while Werner is in the cellar of his hotel. Both have items of value with them: Marie holds on to the Sea of Flames, and Werner has his radio. Part 0 creates a mood of suspense, as the characters await their fate in the bombing. Also, the switch in point of view in each chapter allows the reader to see from multiple perspectives, location-wise as well as internally in the thoughts of the characters. This sets the structure for the rest of the book, which shifts perspective every chapter.

As mentioned in the epigraph, although it is clear at this point in the war that the Germans are losing, Saint-Malo is still a German strong point. The German hold over Saint-Malo it is clearly felt by Werner and by Marie-Laure, the intense nationalism for the Reich still present in the city. Werner notes it in the spirit of the Austrian Detachment, who iare singing while they fire their cannon. Part 0 end with the blinking out of the light in the basement where Werner is, highlighting theme of light and darkness and the motif of vision and seeing. As the bombs come down on the city, the point of view shifts for a moment to Etienne, Marie-Laure's great-uncle, who sees the black dots filling the sky and thinks of the locusts descending, alluding to the Bible.

In the first chapter of Part 1, Marie-Laure is introduced to the myth of the Sea of Flames. Marie-Laure sees the meaning of the allegory more so than anyone else: although she has not yet completely lost her vision, to her the value of her life currently lies in her father, whom she loves and admires. As a demonstration of familial love and loyalty, to her it seems clear to her that the diamond should not be in the hands of a human, because when in possession of the diamond, that holder is endangering those he loves. Marie-Laure's uncanny ability to see more than others around her is demonstrated by this childhood insight. Furthermore, although the myth is told to the children as part of their tour to the museum, they are shown nothing more than a door; thus imagination is required for them to picture the story in their minds.

Part 1 characterizes the protagonists in the way they are as children: curious and imaginative. The narration provides insight into their interests, their personalities, and the people who are important to them. This part also sets the scene for what Marie-Laure and Werner's lives were like before the war. While neither Marie-Laure nor Werner have much economically, both have a life rich in familial love and loyalty, an important theme; through this resource, the characters are able to survive trying times.

The theme of Science and Technology is introduced in both narratives. In Werner's narrative, he and Jutta discover the radio, and he discovers his talent for fixing and using it. In addition, he reads various books and magazines on science, and both he and Jutta begin to tune in to a French broadcast with lectures on science for children—they are especially impressed by the one that details the history of coal. The juxtaposition of darkness and light is poignant in the Frenchman's descriptions: both in the description of the brain that is locked in darkness but creates a world of light, and in the irony of coal, which, coming from the darkness of the earth and burning light in their fire now, may have also absorbed sunlight millions of years ago as a plant. Marie-Laure's science fascination takes place at National Museum of Natural History, a place where she learns she does not have to see in order to discover the magic of science. She can touch and feel textures; she can get lost in the exhibits and be brought safely back to her father. She learns the most under the gentle guidance of Dr. Geffard, who teaches her of the magic of Mollusks. In addition, the theme of imagination and science and technology are displayed in Marie-Laure's love of Jules Verne's novel *Around the World in 80 Days*.

Part 1 builds to a climax as the war looms in Germany and France. Werner and Jutta note that the Deutschland broadcasts, which share nationalist propaganda, overpower almost all of the other broadcasts, beginning to develop the theme of the overpowering nationalism present in Germany in this time period. The nationalism comes with a tone of fear as well, as foreign things are looked down upon. Jutta is inclined to oppose this ideology, questioning why a half-Jewish girl would have been kicked out of the play area, and listening to French broadcasts detailing the bombing of Paris. On the other hand, Werner succumbs to this fear and is inclined to conform to this nationalism, in the end crushing their forbidden radio.

Meanwhile, Marie-Laure's heightened and ironic ability to see what is coming foreshadows Germany's attack on France, as smelled by Marie-Laure in the gasoline underneath the wind. Marie-Laure tries to withdraw into her Jules Verne book and imagination to avoid the reality of the war around her, but is unable to. As she and her father flee Paris, her father also tries to employ the use of imagination to comfort Marie-Laure, but the overall mood surrounding them does not escape her, and she is withdrawn and morose. As this section comes to a close, Daniel LeBlanc reveals that he has one of four versions of the Sea of Flames, possibly the real diamond. Thus the symbolism around it—is this stone shaping his destiny? will it keep him safe, give him eternal life, is it causing the war around them?—comes to question, and the dramatic irony of the reader knowing of the presence of the diamond adds to the suspense of the plot.

All the Light We Cannot See Chapters 32- 61 (Part 2: 8 August 1944 & Part 3: June 1940) Summary and Analysis

Summary

Part 2: 8 August 1944

32: Saint-Malo

The bombs start a fire in Saint-Malo that consumes the city. Doors and roofs are blown off houses and all the books in the library catch fire, as do mattresses and furniture. The beams of houses, some 400 years old, are aflame. The fire is so strong that objects are sucked into the fire. Malouins pray. Some flames are 300 feet high. The hotel of bees becomes almost weightless with fire for a moment and then rains down in little pieces.

33: Number 4 rue Vauborel

Marie-Laure is under her bed clutching the stone and the miniature house when the bombs hit. She feels as if there was a big tree in the center of the town that has been uprooted and is bringing the town with it. She cries out for her father. Then everything gets quiet; she wonders if her uncle, or anyone in the town, has survived. Then she smells the smoke and realizes her bedroom window has broken and there are flames outside. She focuses on breathing and calming herself, and says in French, "this is not reality."

34: Hotel of Bees

In the basement of the Hotel of Bees, Werner remembers the last things he saw before the light went out: Bernd closing the door and Volkheimer turning on his field light. The field light is thrown across the floor as they are all thrown. Werner's mind goes to a time when he was five and watched a miner dig a grave for two dead bony mules; Werner was wondering if the mules had anything left on them that he could eat. Then he is back in the cellar, his hearing buzzing, weights on top of him; he can't hear himself speak, and when he tries to get up the ceiling is low. He picks hot pieces of rock off of himself. The room heats up, and he feels like they are in a box thrown inside a volcano. Everything is black but for little wisps of red and blue light. He asks, "Are we dead?"

35: Down Six Flights

Marie-Laure realizes she has to go into the cellar. She replaces the stone in the miniature house and puts the little house in her pocket. She finds her cane but cannot find her shoes, so she goes in stockings. She counts her steps between locations as she descends the 6 floors, stopping to use the bathroom, stopping to drink water out of the full bathtub, and making sure that she isn't walking into any areas with fires. She puts on her uncle's wool coat, grabs half a loaf of bread and opens the cellar door on the floor of the kitchen. She notes the strong smell of stranded shellfish in the cellar, which is contrasted with the smell of fire from outside. She enters the cellar and closes the door.

36: Trapped

Werner sees Volkheimer scanning his field light over the wreckage. He sees twisted shelves and a pile of rubble that he realizes used to be the stairs. He watches Volkheimer go over to a pile of rubble and dismantle it, finding Bernd underneath, covered in dust, eyes voids, mouth open, but Werner cannot hear screaming or anything over the sound in his ears. Volkheimer sets Bernd in a yellow armchair that's still standing, then comes over to Werner. He touches Werner's cheeks and his fingers come away red. Werner says that they have to get out, and he watches Volkheimer's lips say that there is no other way out.

Part 3: June 1940

37: Château

Marie-Laure and her father arrive in Evreux, which is a bleak sight: a man lying face down near market stalls; the latest newspaper 36 hours old. Arriving at Monsieur Giannott's house they find it burning and being looted by young boys. The house was a grand château. One boy tells them that Monsieur Giannott fled to London. Marie-Laure's feet hurt and she can't walk anymore, so her father carries her on his back. He takes her to an abandoned barn and picks the lock to get in. He pretends to Marie-Laure that the barn is a hotel, that it smells of horses because a guest just brought horses in the lobby. Monsieur Leblanc gathers vegetables from a garden and feeds Marie-Laure. She asks if they are going to great uncle Etienne's house, the uncle who her father says is 76% crazy. Her father says Etienne is crazy because he saw Marie's grandfather die in the war, and got "gas in the brain" so he sees things that aren't there. Outside, it starts to rain.

38: Entrance Exam

Werner goes to the Entrance Exam for the National Political Institutes of Education with 100 other boys, held in a dance hall in Essen decorated with War ministry flags. They are told they are applying to enter the most elite schools in the world. They are all given white uniforms. He takes a test that has more to do with his genes and his family history than with his knowledge. They are also subjected to physical tests, where examiners watch them like livestock. After each day, the other boys are picked up by family members; he stays at a hostel. He thinks of Frau Elena, who said she was proud of him in a dazed way as she sent him off, and of Jutta, who hasn't spoken to him since he smashed their radio. The next day he has raciological exams of his size and hair color and eye color, which are matched on a scale of other's colors. His hair is the lightest, the color of snow. His vision is tested as well, and then there are verbal exams on their knowledge of history and politics. He continues to think of Jutta and how she acts as if he betrayed her. Day 3 is more physical tests, including jumping and running. On the last day, the very last test requires the boys to climb to a platform and then jump down into a flag held by the other boys. The first boy who goes hesitates at the top, then seems to faint and fall sideways down, almost missing the flag, and breaking his arm. When Werner goes he knows he must be strong. He thinks of how they will only take the purest; he also thinks of how he will be put to work in the mines if he does not make it. He climbs up and, without hesitating, jumps down and lands in the center of the flag; he gets up uninjured, yelling "*Heil* Hitler" and making eye contact with the examiner.

39: Brittany

Marie-Laure and her father get a ride in the truck bed of a furniture truck, with others who are fleeing. No one has seen a German yet. Marie-Laure hopes that all of this has been an elaborate test by her father and that they are really headed back to Paris, and all will return to normal. When they are close to Saint-Malo the truck runs out of gas. Marie-Laure walks part of the way and her father carries her the rest of the way. When they enter Saint-Malo her father narrates what he sees in the city of walls. She suspects that although he makes it sound new and magical, it is actually frightening. They arrive on the street of her uncle, which is completely dark and without people. It is the middle of the night. They ring the bell of the house three times and then rest. Monsieur LeBlanc pulls out his last cigarette to smoke. They hear footsteps inside.

40: Madame Manec

A woman named Madame Manec lets Marie-Laure and Monsieur LeBlanc into the house. She is astonished by their presence there, but quickly gets to work making them food. Marie-Laure observes the sounds of the kitchen, and Madame Manec's heavy shoes walking the floor. Marie-Laure finds Madame Manec's laughter and low voice kind. Marie-Laure is overpowered by the delicious smell of an omelette cooking. After, she eats canned peaches, two jars full. The adults talk of Etienne, the great uncle, and how he is doing. Monsieur Leblanc is grateful that Madame Manec offers him a cigarette. Marie-Laure can hear the sounds of the ocean outside, and thinks of how she is on the edge of Brittany, the edge of France. She drifts off to sleep.

41: You Have Been Called

Werner returns home and all of the children ask him what his experience was like, what he learned, and whether he got to fire rifles. With the money leftover from Herr Seidler he buys a new radio, one that can only receive Deutschland broadcasts (broadcasts from the state). Jutta has not spoken to Werner since he broke their radio, and she does not speak much to him when he gets back. Five days after his returns, Werner receives an official envelope stating that he has been called: he will go to

Schulpforta. He shows the letter to Frau Elena and she states that the people here will be happy—but Jutta will not be happy. Townspeople come to congratulate Werner and read his letter. Jutta comes back to the house after an excursion with other girls and Frau Elena shares the news. Jutta immediately runs upstairs. A young boy named Siegfried shows Werner a picture of men flying airplanes, their scarves blown back by the wind; he says to Werner, "you'll show them won't you." Werner agrees, "absolutely I will."

42: Occuper

Marie-Laure wakes up to the sound of church bells and realizes she has slept most of the day. She looks for her cane and cannot find it. She calls "hello" out the door of her room. She explores the room; it has a tall window and a dresser. She can hear a roar that sounds like a crowd, but she wonders if it's the ocean. She notes she can feel the weather between her fingers. Madame Manec comes upstairs and leads Marie-Laure to the bed, and offers her a bath. Monsieur Leblanc went to see if he can send a telegram, but Madame Manec doubts he will be able to. She tells Marie-Laure she has worked at the house since Etienne was a child. Marie-Laure asks about her great-uncle Etienne, how he can afford the house (he inherited it), and where he is. He is on the 5th floor and never leaves the house. Madame Manec says the war changed Etienne and he does not feel safe outside the house. Marie-Laure stands on the bed, touches the window, and asks if the ocean is outside. Madame Manec agrees to open the shutters even though they are supposed to remain closed. Marie-Laure wants to know if there are snails in the sea; Madame Manec says there are. Marie-Laure is delighted because she has found snails on land but never in the sea. At dinner that night they listen to the radio, which lists off people who are trying to find or send messages to their loved ones. Her father says that no telegraphs are going out, and that the latest newspaper is 6 days old. Madame Manec switches off the radio but Marie-Laure thinks she still hears the radio coming from somewhere else. After dinner Marie-Laure and her father settle into the same bed. Her father tells her that the Germans are occupying France. She asks him questions about what this means: will they have to speak German? Are the Germans using their beds in Paris? She says that she hopes they can go back to their apartment in Paris and everything will be where it was. Her father does not reassure her.

43: Don't Tell Lies

Werner cannot concentrate on his chores. He has lots of thoughts about what is happening next, and is also feeling some doubt, which he does not like because he feels this is his moment of escape. He prepares an argument to convince Jutta, but Jutta avoids talking to him. Finally on his last day he wakes at dawn and goes to Jutta's bed, where she is twisted inside her blanket in sleep. Above her are the drawings she has done. He wakes her and asks her to walk with him. She agrees. They walk to an area on a canal where they used to watch ice skaters race in the winter. He used to love the exhilaration of watching them speed by, but afterwards he would feel lonely and trapped in his life. He can hear the coal mine pounding away and can see the soot. He says to Jutta that the ice skaters did not come last year. She replies that they will not come this year either. She tells Werner that she used to listen to the radio from Paris on their little radio, and that in Paris they said the opposite of what Deutschland is saying: they are saying that Germany is committing atrocities. Jutta states that Werner will become like the other mean boys at the Children's House who joined the Hitler Youth. Werner says he will not be that way. Jutta is not convinced. "Is it right," she asks, "to do something only because everyone else is doing it?" Werner feels doubt again. He tells Jutta he will be able to take her on a plane and fly her to parts of Germany she hasn't been to. She says, "don't tell lies." Ten hours later he is on the train.

44: Etienne

On the 3rd day that Marie-Laure is at Etienne' house, she finds snail shells, known as "whelks" (from her lessons with Dr. Geffard), outside her room. The shells lead in a path toward the door of her great-uncle Etienne. He invites her in and takes her hand. He apologizes for not being able to meet her sooner. She expects his room to smell musty, but it smells like soap and books. He has the entire floor to himself, with two windows facing the street and two facing the back. She can hear radio coming from all sides of the room, and he has her touch all of his 11 radios. He also demonstrates paperweights, a matchbox full of beetles, and fuses for his radio. He has many books. Although he does not own anything by Jules Verne, he does have Darwin. He begins to read aloud from a book, translating from English to French as he goes. Madame Manec brings sandwiches. Marie-Laure feels her uncle is kind and very sane. Marie-Laure feels warm, drowsing on the Davenport, listening to her uncle read.

At the telegraph office Monsieur Leblanc watches two German motorcycles, a black Mercedes, and two trucks approach the Chateau Saint-Malo, where the mayor awaits them. Twelve Germans emerge from the vehicles, looking tidy, with shiny boots, and one man in a field captain uniform approaches and enters the chateau. He speaks with the mayor through his aide de camp. They go to a second-floor window, unfurl a red flag, and secure it there.

45: Jungmänner

Werner arrives at his new school, which is a series of large stone buildings that remind him of castles. The air is pure and dust-free. He is given his various uniforms and told the strict rules. There are 400 recruits, ages 9-19. They will all carry a knife, and all learn to use a Mauser rifle. The boy in the bunk above Werner is named Frederick; he is from Berlin and knows a lot about birds, often watching and identifying birds out their dorm window. Werner is fascinated by all the equipment in the science labs. They have classes in phrenology (the study of skull size in relation to character), in which they discuss the purity of the German race. They also learn literature, history, science, and many other topics, in addition to the extreme physical training they do. Some of the other cadets come from rich families, or are sons of ministers, and talk in a slang that Werner has never heard before. He wants to belong; he has never before been a part of something so single-minded. They are like mounds of clay being molded into the same shape. There is a picture of the führer in every classroom. Werner focuses on memorizing routes to classrooms and lyrics to the nationalist songs.

46: Vienna

Sergeant Major Reinhold von Rumpel is a Nazi in France, who is a specialist in gems. He is 40 and married, with two daughters, and he has been away from his family on duty for 2 months. Before the war he worked as a gemologist, evaluating gems and faceting diamonds. Now, he has been charged with the task of documenting the goods of value that the Nazis have found in France, such as a set of dishes with a diamond set on the border of each one. He takes these items, boxes them, labels them, and places them in a train car with 24-hour guards. The rumor is that the führer is collecting precious objects from all over Europe. Today von Rumpel is in a geological library in Vienna reading about the history of gems of cultural value that have existed in Europe. As he sits there reading, when he crosses his legs he notices a slight swelling that troubles his groin. He specifically is looking for the Sea of Flames.

47: Boches

Monsieur Leblanc says the Germans have shiny boots and weapons that look as if they have never been used. The mayor tells them the country is in mourning; they are not allowed to dance and they cannot go out on the streets at night. The women who come in and out of Madame Manec's kitchen tell of the Germans, or *Boches*, who buy postcards, candies, champagne, cheese, and butter. Marie-Laure feels like her life in Paris was interrupted in a parallel to her book *Twenty Thousand Leagues Under the Sea*. She asks her father if she can go out, and he tells her no. She asks why they have to sleep in that small room, and not in the bigger room across the hall; they aren't sleeping there because that room belonged to her grandfather. Marie-Laure spends time learning the layout of the house. The first floor is Madame Manec's, and the kitchen is there. The second floor has an old sewing room and maid's room. The third is full of junk, things Marie-Laure can't always identify. The fourth floor has more clutter, along with antique doll houses built by her grandfather. The fifth floor is all Etienne's. The 6th floor has the small room where Marie-Laure and her father sleep, the toilet, and her grandfather's room. Madame Manec's friends who visit tell stories of people eating pets and pigeons in Paris, where things are very quiet at night and people have their car headlights painted blue.

48: Hauptmann

Dr. Hauptmann, instructor of technical science, gives all the cadets a box of parts, copper wire, a battery, screws, a sheet of metal, and other items, all parts newer and nicer than Werner has ever seen. He draws a simple circuit on the board and asks them to make it. Werner concentrates and is able to construct one quickly. Then, the professor notices Werner, tests the circuit, which works, and asks the class to make a motor. Werner constructs one in 15 seconds. The Teacher, a small man with almost translucent eyelids, watches Werner closely and asks him what else he can make. Weber lists a few items—a doorbell, an ohmmeter—and is told to make them all.

49: Flying Couch

Notices go up in the town that everyone must surrender their firearms or be shot. Farmers, hunters, and olds sailors come and surrender theirs in a truck that drives away. Monsieur Leblanc smokes constantly, and builds a model of Saint-Malo for Marie-Laure. She feels anxious about this because she does not want to stay in Saint-Malo. Marie-Laure visits her uncle in his room, where they play "flying couch." They sit on the Davenport and decide where they will travel to—Borneo, New York City, the moon—with her uncle narrating their adventure and adding details of smells and tastes of things like "moon flesh" (cheese). At the end of the adventure they pat the couch cushions and arrive home.

50: The Sum of Angles

Werner is called to Dr. Hauptmann laboratory. There he is greeted by long-legged greyhound dogs. He enters a room full of books, and is directed to add a log to the fire. He sees another cadet in the corner, 17-year-old Frank Volkheimer, who is known for his strength and his toughness. Dr. Hauptmann shows Werner a formula, and asks him to use it, giving him numbers to plug in. Werner concentrates on the formula and produces a correct result. Dr. Hauptmann says Werner will work in the laboratory every night, and Volkheimer will watch out for him. Finally, he tells Werner to breathe, saying that he can't hold his breath the entire time he's in his laboratory. He gives Werner a box of biscuits. Back in his bunk, Werner shares a biscuit with Frederick. Frederick reports he saw an eagle owl outside. Other boys urge them not to talk because the bunk master is coming. Werner imagines himself receiving a prize in a white labcoat. Werner listens to the terrified breathing of his dorm mates.

51: The Professor

One day while Marie-Laure and her uncle are reading Darwin, he stops and says that someone is there. She does not hear anyone at all. Etienne goes down to the kitchen, and Marie-Laure follows him. In the kitchen he opens a door in the floor that leads to a cellar, and tells her to hurry and step down. Marie-Laure is concerned there may be danger. Madame Manec comes and tells her nothing is wrong, and he tells Etienne not to scare Marie-Laure. Marie-Laure sits with Etienne in the cellar. His breathing is shallow and frightened. She asks why he does not go outside. He says it is because big spaces scare him. She reminds him that things he likes come from outside, such as the food from their lunch. He reads more of their Darwin book, and then suddenly she asks him what is behind in the locked door in her grandfather's room. He takes her upstairs and unlocks the door. Inside, a passage leads to the garret, which has a tangle of equipment and cables. This is Etienne's radio broadcasting studio. He broadcasts recordings that he and his brother made together; Etienne wrote the scripts about science, and his brother read them, because his voice was always admired. They originally were trying to sell the recordings to a studio in Paris, but later the studio lost interest. Etienne would broadcast the ten recordings, along with a Debussy piano song of his brother's, every night. Marie-Laure asks if any of the songs ever reached children, and Etienne does not know. However, Etienne admits he was not trying to reach children: he was trying to play them to his deceased brother. Marie-Laure asked if his brother ever responded, and he says no.

In between Chapters 51 and 52:

In a series of letters to his sister, Werner tells her of his work in the laboratory of Dr. Hauptmann, who is said to be connected with someone powerful, but part of the letter is redacted. Dr. Hauptmann tells Werner that the führer is collecting scientists to control the weather, and to send a rocket to Japan. Werner talks of how he is respected because Frank Volkheimer, or 'the giant', is with him. He tells a story of a national hero, Reiner Schicker, who was caught, tortured, and killed by the enemy; before he died, he said he regretted that he only could give one life for his country. Frederick has a comment about the story that Werner reports, but it is redacted. In another letter Werner tells of a hunting expedition in the woods, where Frederick returned with a shirt full of berries and ripped sleeves. He sends his wishes for Jutta and Frau Elena's coughs to improve.

52: Perfumer

Claude Levitte, known as Big Claude, owns a parfumerie on the rue Vauborel, the same street where Etienne lives. Although Claude doesn't usually earn much in his perfumería, lately he has been making money by paying farmers to butcher their stock, and he takes the meat to Paris via train to sell it at a high price. Doing this he has to pay off authorities and be strategic. On this day he is in his shop watching the German soldiers outside pass. He admires their efficiency, even though he knows he should resent them. He sees "the Parisian" (monsieur Leblanc) come out of Etienne's house and walk down the street to the corner, behind the Germans, looking up at buildings and taking notes. Claude feels that the occupation authorities will want to know about this, and takes note himself.

53: Time of the Ostriches

Marie-Laure counts the days since she has been allowed to go outside—121. She thinks of the radio signal crossing over oceans and reaching people all over the world. She hears stories in Madame Manec's kitchen of Parisian cousins writing to ask for hams and hens; meanwhile the parfumerie is smuggling meat to Paris, and the dentist is selling wine via mail. Monsieur Leblanc continues to build the model. She asks him if she can go outside, even just on his arm, but he says no. She thinks of the boys in Paris who told her the Nazis would take the blind girls first. The mayor announces a new tax, and people say he has abandoned them. It's the time of the ostriches, but Marie-Laure wants to know which ones—the German or the French—are the ones with their heads in the sand. Madame Manec falls asleep now at the kitchen table, climbs the stairs slowly, and during the day takes food out to the less fortunate.

54: Weakest

Bastian is the officer in charge of field exercises; he wears hobnailed boots and seems capable of great violence in Werner's eyes. He tells the cadets that they must drive the weak parts out of the corps, just like they are driving out the weakness from their bodies. Bastian picks one kid, Bäcker, and asks him to choose the weakest one in the corps. Werner holds his breath, worried that he'll be chosen because he is the smallest. Instead he chooses a slow runner named Ernst. The officer tells Ernst that he must race to the place where the officer is standing with a 10-second head-start. Then, the rest of the 60 boys have to try to catch up to Ernst before he reaches the officer. Werner stays in the middle of the pack as the boys gain on Ernst, knowing what will happen if they catch him. They gain on him and some boys begin to grab for him, but at the last moment Ernst reaches the officer.

55: Mandatory Surrender

A notice is issued in Saint-Malo that all people must surrender their radios or risk imprisonment. Etienne stays locked in the room Henri (his brother) while Madame Manec and Monsieur Leblanc pack up the radios. Some of the radios are very large or very old—Etienne had one of them specially shipped to him from the USA in 1921. Marie-Laure asks what the Germans will do with the radios. Her father says, they will send them to Germany; Madame Manec says they will pitch them in the sea. Even after they've taken the last radio and Monsieur Leblanc has carted them all, in 3 trips, to surrender them, Etienne does not come out. Marie-Laure wonders if the radio transmitter counts as a radio, and also realizes that her father and Madame Manec must not know about it.

56: Museum

Sergeant Major Reinhold von Rumpel is in Paris, where he goes to the National Museum and asks, in French, to be shown the gems. He is introduced to the assistant director, and to a mineralogist named Professor Hublin. Von Rumpel is impressed by the collection, and by the amount of treasures they left behind. When they have finished showing him the collection, he asks to see the collections that are not on public display. The assistant director and Professor Hublin exchange a look and state that they have shown him all they are allowed to show him. They go to the assistant director's office, and von Rumpel tells them he is specifically interested in a specimen that he believes has been recently brought out of the vaults. He states that he is very patient, and will wait to be shown the items they are not allowed to show him. He does not allow them to answer the door or the phone. Hours pass. Von Rumpel takes out his lunch of bread and cheese, and eats it without offering them any. Professor Hublin stands the entire time, although von Rumpel encourages him to sit. The assistant director takes out a manuscript and reads it, taking notes. As evening approaches, von Rumpel observes that the two men must be thinking of their children, who are getting out of school at this hour and will need to walk home alone. Von Rumpel knows the schools where the children go, and their ages. Von Rumpel tells them he knows the diamond is not in the museum, but that he wants to see where it was kept. He also says to Professor Hublin that perhaps he believes the myth around the stone. Hublin anxiously asks if their children are safe; von Rumpel replies that the children are safe if their parents wish them to be. Finally the assistant director declares that he's had enough, and calls in Sylvie, a woman who comes and brings them keys. Von Rumpel is surprised that his method worked so quickly—he feels he could have waited for days. The assistant director and Professor Hublin take von Rumpel to the back of the main floor, where behind a door they go down a corkscrewing stone staircases, through hallways and past a warder who drops his newspaper and stares. They reach an unassuming supply room with a simple safe, inside of which there is a second heavy box, with no apparent hinges or nails—it is just a block of polished wood. A key is inserted and two more key holes open on the opposite side. They unlock perhaps 5 shafts, until the box falls open and reveals a small felt bag. Von Rumpel directs them to open it, and the assistant director does, taking out a blue stone as big as a pigeon's egg.

57: The Wardrobe

There is a blackout order: no one can have lights on during certain hours. However, the hotel where the Germans stay has lamps on at all hours of the night. Marie-Laure hears her uncle finally leave his brother's room in the night, and she goes to him to inform him of what has happened to his radios. She hears him go into his room and feel his empty shelves, reciting nursery rhymes to himself. She goes to him and leads him to the Davenport, she can feel his fear. She tells him she that she did not tell her father and Madame Manec about the transmitter in the attic. He suggests they turn it in, but the deadline was yesterday. Without using any light, they go into her grandfather's room. Etienne uses an automobile jack to lift each side of the heavy wardrobe and place rags underneath the feet. Then, they move the wardrobe in front of the door that goes to the attic.

58: Blackbirds

Werner continues working at Dr. Hauptmann's lab, calculating triangles as a way of improving the power of a directional radio transmitter he is building. Sometimes Dr. Hauptmann is talkative, and other days he is eerily quiet. Werner admires Dr. Hauptmann's power: he has connections in high places. Jutta and Werner continue to exchange letters; he is not sure if she has forgiven him, and sometimes her letters have so many parts censored that they do not make sense. Volkheimer continues to watch over Werner. The other boys see him as The Giant, a brute, but Werner sees another side of him: when Dr. Hauptmann is not in the lab, Volkheimer will bring in a radio and play classical music. Werner wonders why Hauptmann needs him to calculate so many triangles. Hauptmann tells him to think of it as pure science. Werner tries to discuss his theories with Frederick, but Frederick is distracted and constantly chatting about birds. Ernst, the boy who was chosen as the weakest, leaves the school, as do two others, making the group of 60 into 57. Winter is coming and birds begin to migrate. Some of the older cadets sometimes practice firing their guns into the trees to watch the birds scatter, which Frederick hates. Werner does everything alongside Frederick, and seems to be watching out for him.

At the end of the chapter a telegram is displayed, December 10 1940, a duplicate of a telephoned telegram, with a message to M. Daniel LeBlanc: "Return to Paris end of month = travel securely=."

59: Bath

Daniel LeBlanc has finished the model of Saint-Malo. It is not perfect, made of different woods and lacking detail, but it will do to help Marie-Laure know the city if needed. He is concerned about the telegram he received directing him to come back to Paris, and he isn't sure if the message means he should bring the stone and Marie-Laure. He buys his train ticket and notices the man from the parfumerie watching him. Madame Manec says he is not to be trusted. Daniel has convinced himself that it is possible he holds the real stone: he has tested it in various ways, trying to scratch it with quartz, burying it in a flower bed, boiling it; he is concerned it has caused Marie-Laure and France bad luck, but feels idiotic for thinking so. On his last night before leaving he helps Marie-Laure with her bath, and washes her hair for her. He thinks of how he always felt he might be missing something as a parent, something that mothers on the streets in Paris seemed to know. He also feels very proud that he has been able to raise her alone, and that she has such curiosity and such resilience. She asks him if he is leaving. He tells her he will not be gone more than ten days. He brushes her hair after her bath, and she reviews the model of Saint-Malo. She asks if they have ever spent a night apart, and he says they have not.

60: Weakest (#2)

Winter begins at Werner's school, the "castle" building of the school growing darker, and the cleanest snow that Werner has ever seen falling, free of coal dust. Two corporals come every few weeks to tell a cadet his father has been killed in action. Sometimes Bastian comes in and asks them if they are Homesick, and reminds them that all will go home to the führer in the end. Despite the cold and the snow, they continue their exercises with Bastian. On this day, he asks a boy named Helmut Rodel to choose the weakest; he chooses Frederick. Bastian asks Frederick if he is the weakest, Frederick replies he does not know. As Bastian gives Frederick his 10-second head-start, Frederick is distracted and and does not run right away. The other boys—some of them fast as greyhounds, harvested for their speed—catch up to Frederick before Frederick reaches the commandant. Bastian gives Helmut a long black rubber hose, and has him beat Frederick with it. While Werner watches his friend being beaten, he tries to focus on comforting memories from home, memories including Frau Elena and Jutta. Werner does not feel Frederick is weak: he is able to do many things that Werner is not. When the beating ends, Frederick is facedown in the snow. Werner rolls him over and sees that his face is bloody, one eye is swollen shut, and the other eye looks into the sky, following a hawk. Bastian tells Frederick to get up, and asks him if he is the weakest, to which he replies, "No, sir." The group of boys continues running, singing a song, their rifles bouncing against their backs. Werner is almost 15 years old.

61: The Arrest of the Locksmith

Daniel LeBlanc is arrested when he is a few hours from Paris. He is questioned, first by French investigators and later by German ones, about his keys and locksmith tools, and about why he was noting the size of the buildings in Saint-Malo. They seem to be accusing him of plotting to destroy Chateau de Saint-Malo. In his jail cell they do not give him cigarettes, linens, or access to a telephone. He believes the museum will come rescue him and explain. He is imprisoned with some other French, Belgians, Flemings, and Walloons. They only talk vaguely of what they are accused of. After four days they are brought to Germany, over the river, which Daniel notes does not seem much different.

Analysis

Part 2 brings the reader into the immediate aftermath of the bombings, focusing on the point of view of Werner and Marie-Laure as they get their bearings. In Marie-Laure's narrative of the bombing, a simile is employed to compare the event to an uprooting of a huge tree. Marie-Laure is miraculously safe in the top floor of her house, while other houses around her burn; not coincidentally, she also holds the Sea of Flames in her hands. True to the allegory of the Sea of Flames, it seems to Marie-Laure that alone in her house, she could be the only one surviving. Marie-Laure calls out to her father, "Papa," repeatedly, invoking the theme of familial devotion that has been a strengthening force for her. At the same time, she tries to use the power of her imagination to escape by telling herself that "This is not reality."

Meanwhile, where Werner is trapped in the basement with Volkheimer, the narration uses imagery through a metaphor, "We are locked inside a box, and the box has been pitched into the mouth of a volcano." Werner gets pulled into a memory of a bleak scene where he watched a miner dig a grave for two dead mules. As he comes to, he realizes he is in a parallel nightmare: he, Bernd, and Volkheimer are trapped inside the cellar. True to the familial love and loyalty developed between the members of Werner's team, Volkheimer is doing what he can to ensure the safety of both Bernd and Werner. Just as the suspense of the fire and being trapped, Doerr switches from August 1944 back to June 1940, thus building the momentum of the story.

Part 3 emphasizes theme of nationalism in Germany, especially in regard to racial purity. Werner is enticed by the ideology presented to him; this is because he wants to succeed, to belong to something, and to escape from his own fate in the coal mines. The ideology is sold to him as cruel and intolerant of impurity, and although Werner watches other boys suffer, his only thought is that he must not fail. At the same time, his family loyalty pulls at him: Frau Elena's lack of enthusiasm for his achievements, and Jutta's feeling that he has betrayed her. Werner is striving to be pure by the Nazi standards, enduring cruelty in the name of the nation. In contrast, Jutta's characterization appears as the truly pure one of the two, as when she asks Werner, "Is it right to do something only because everyone else is doing it?"

Once at Schulpforta, the narration employs metaphor and similes for how the boys are being inundated with propaganda. For example, one simile compares the boys to mounds of clay being molded into the same shape; another simile compares them to greyhounds, trained to run quickly. Even the purity of the setting of Schulpforta emphasizes the sub-theme of purity, with Werner continuously noting how dust free and pure the air is, and how clean the snow is. To strengthen their nationalism and oneness, nationalist songs sung during exercises use metaphor to frame the boys as the weapons defending their country. As the cruelty intensifies, Werner sees his friend Frederick subjected to the "Who's the weakest?" test that the commandant Bastian has set up. Werner feels he can do nothing to help Frederick, so he retreats into memories of Jutta and Frau Elena—using his key source of strength, that of the familial love he has, and leaving Frederick to fend for himself. Despite these obvious cruelties, Werner shies away from doing anything to compromise his own status as the scientific prodigy of the cruel Dr. Hauptmann. Werner works closely with Volkheimer, and they start to develop a close relationship of an almost brother-like nature; Volkheimer protects him, and Werner looks up to Volkheimer in many ways, which is apparent as he writes Jutta letters full of nationalist stories, as if he were trying to believe them himself.

Marie-Laure and her father arrive in Saint-Malo, and her father once again uses imagination as escape, to try to describe the city in a magical way to Marie-Laure, and he also carries her. His love for her and her survival and comfort are his top priorities, even as he carries what could be a very valuable jewel. Madame Manec is characterized as kind and warm, continuing the theme of familial loyalty: she does not question Daniel and Marie-Laure's presence there, and immediately takes them in.

Etienne, who is at first only characterized as being traumatized by the first World War, is introduced to Marie-Laure, and her view of him is more more nuanced than the person her father and Madame Manec described to her. Ironically, she can see more in Etienne than the adults around her can see: she sees his adventurous, intelligent, sane side, something that he shares genuinely. Etienne's room is like a shrine to Science and Technology, as he has 11 radios and countless collections of items, such as beetles and books. The magic of science appears to live in the room of Etienne, as well as in his broadcasting tower in the attic of his 6th floor home. This room sets the scene for more imaginative travel for Marie-Laure, this time at the mercy of the Davenport, the couch in Etienne's study, and Etienne's wild narratives.

Overlap of Werner and Marie-Laure's narratives becomes clearer as Marie-Laure learns of the recordings Etienne used to broadcast in the night, hearing a short sentence from one about coal burning—a repetition of the same broadcast the reader saw Werner and Jutta tune into. There is dramatic irony in this moment, as the reader knows the source of the broadcast but Werner and Jutta still do not know the source of their one-time favorite broadcast.

Von Rumpel, the primary antagonist, is very exacting and patient in his methods of seeking the Sea of Flames; in the scene where he sits with the assistant director and professor, waiting for them to show him what they have, he hears in his head the advice of his father about being patient. Thus, the antagonist is also motivated and strengthened by the themes of familial love and memory. These chapters also introduce a foil to Daniel LeBlanc: Claude Levitte, a fat, unsavory, and selfish perfumer who is a collaborator with the Germans, one of the causes of Daniel LeBlanc's imprisonment. Claude stands in physical contrast to Daniel, who is tall and thin with a loving and kind character.

Daniel LeBlanc is worried about whether the curse of the diamond stands, and conducted various tests on it: pulling in the theme of science as a way of discovering magic. Part 3 ends in suspense, as Daniel LeBlanc is imprisoned, thus continuing the momentum of the story, and bringing into question the "truth" behind the curse of the stone—a stone that, in a show of dramatic irony, the reader knows is in the possession of Marie-Laure.

All the Light We Cannot See Analysis Chapters 62-95 (Part 4: 8 August 1944 & Part 5: January 1941) Summary and Analysis

Summary

Part 4: 8 August 1944

62: The Fort of La Cité

Von Rumpel climbs a ladder to a tower that looks out on the city of Saint-Malo, half a mile away, as it burns. He struggles climbing the ladder because of his swollen lymph nodes that make it hard for him to breathe. The two soldiers in the turret look out at the burning city, observing various things, such as the disappearance of the church spire. Von Rumpel looks at the fire through binoculars, trying to locate the tall house on rue Vauborel (Etienne's home), which he sees has not burned. Von Rumpel returns to the fort below, where he sits with other soldiers and eats a tube of cheese. The colonel in charge has told them they will still beat the Americans, that reinforcements will come. Von Rumpel thinks of his swollen groin and his swollen lymph nodes, imagining a black rope has grown inside him and will choke his heart. He thinks of how he will wait until the fire dies down and then enter the house.

63: Atelier de Réparation

Bernd the engineer squirms in pain in the chair, something wrong with his leg and his chest. Werner's hearing begins to come back in his right ear, but not in his left. The radio has been damaged and does not work. Volkheimer tries to unblock the stairway, turning his field light off and on again to try to conserve the battery, saying "Please" out loud as he works. Werner thinks the fire should have sucked out all of the air from the cellar by now, but it has not. The cellar used to be a corsair's, then a place to store gold, then a room to do repairs, reparations, Atelier de Réparations; Werner thinks this is appropriate, as there are people who will think these three men have reparations to make.

64: Two Cans

Marie-Laure wakes up in the cellar, sweating in her uncle's coat, with the small model house pinned below her. She does not hear anything outside; she wonders if the fire brigade is out there, or the Americans. She wants to go check, but then worries that the Germans might still hold the city. She thinks of where Etienne might be—coming back to the house, or plagued by his demons, or dead. She tries not to finish the loaf of bread, but she does because she is famished. She wishes she brought her novel. She explores the cellar, and in one corner she finds two full cans. She has memories of Madame Manec's canning of peaches; she remembers her fingers sticky. She hopes that the cans contain peaches, or some other food, rather than oil. She tries not to think of her bladder. She thinks of Foucault's pendulum, and how she saw it at the Panthéon in Paris with her father when she was 8 or 9. She thinks of how the pendulum always swings, thus proving the movement of the world, and how it will keep swinging forever. She feels that she can hear the pendulum swinging in front of her now.

65: Number 4 rue Vauborel

Von Rumpel makes his way through Saint-Malo, limping. He sees shreds of different items, like a flower box and a dead horse. No one warns him away from mines. A schnauzer follows him briefly, and he only sees one other person—a woman holding a dustpan outside of what used to be the movie theater. On rue Vauborel, many roof tiles have fallen onto the street. He thinks of how he will enter the house, even if it burned, and pluck the diamond from the ashes. He reaches Number 4 and sees the list of occupants on the door: M. Etienne LeBlanc, age 63, and Mlle. Marie-Laure Leblanc, age 16. He thinks of the dangers he is willing to endure for the Third Reich; no one stops him from entering.

66: What They Have

Volkheimer tries to make Bernd drink from his canteen. In Werner's duffel he has his childhood notebook, his blanket, socks, and three rations, the only food they have. They also have two half-empty canteens of water, and the sludgy water at the bottom of a bucket of brushes. Volkheimer has two grenades in his pocket, which Bernd urges him to use to explode them out—however, with the rubble, 8-millimeter shells, and close quarters, this would be suicide. Volkheimer has his rifle with 5 rounds; Werner thinks they would only need three, one bullet for each. Werner feels he can see somewhat in the dark of the cellar, that the dark is not completely dark. The white dust inside this cellar is like the inverse of the coal dust of his home town: his being trapped there like a parallel or inverse of his father being trapped in the coal mine. Volkheimer asks Werner about the radio, which Werner thinks is hopeless. He tells Werner they are running out of time, that life is worth living, and to think of his sister.

67: Trip Wire

Marie-Laure leaves the basement to relieve herself in the bedpan in Madame Manec's room. She wonders if she should leave the house, and she wishes she could talk to her father. She finds a knife in the kitchen, and a brick, to open the cans. She tells herself that if no one has come by the time she finishes the cans, and if her uncle has not come home, she will go look for someone. She drinks from the bathtub on the third floor, then sits and positions herself to open the cans, but before she does, the trip wire behind her alerts her that someone has entered the house.

Part 5: January 1941

68: January Recess

Before the boys of the Schulpforta school leave for January recess, the commandant makes a speech to them about the emblematic fire they carry wherever they go. Frederick's face still has bruises from his beating. He invites Werner home to Berlin with him for the break; Frederick's mother pays the way. They take a train together to Berlin. It's the biggest city Werner has ever seen. He thinks of all of the scientific discoveries made here, like x-rays and plastic. In Frederick's apartment building there is an elevator, and Werner asks to ride it again and again, until a woman, Frau Schwartzenberger, enters the building and also gets on. She is a Jew, indicated by the yellow star on her collar. The boys ride the elevator with her, and finally get out on the second floor, while the "Jewess" continues to the 5th floor. A maid named Fanni answers the door and welcomes them in. Frederick's home is full of thick carpet that absorbs sound. He goes into a room and puts on thick glasses; he says to Werner that he must have known about his poor eyesight. Werner isn't sure he did, and Frederick reminds him of how he missed the target in marksmanship, and tells Werner how he memorized the eye charts and calibrated his binoculars to his eyes. Frederick's face relaxes with his glasses on, and Werner thinks that this is how Frederick really is. Fanni feeds them cheese and bread. Frederick shows Werner his two-volume set of books filled with colorful bird paintings done by Audubon, an American ornithologist. The books are forbidden because they are not German, so they are hidden on a top shelf. Frederick's mother comes home, observes his bruises, and welcomes Werner. They sit at the table and drink wine, and Frederick's mother tells a story about a famous tennis player she met on the street. She puts makeup over Frederick's bruises and takes the two of them to a bistro, a restaurant so fancy that Werner never would have imagined eating there. Werner feels warm from the wine. While there, women come by to greet Frederick's mother, ask after her husband, and talk to the boys. Werner overhears Frederick's mother telling one woman that the "Schwartzenberger crone" will be gone by the end of the year, and then they will have the top floor. Werner feels very uneasy; the restaurant suddenly feels overcrowded. Frederick asks if he is all right. After dinner they walk home and go to bed. Werner sleeps in a trundle bed that Frederick's mother has apologized for, but it is the most comfortable bed Werner has ever slept in. Before they sleep, Werner asks Frederick if he sometimes wishes he didn't have to go back; Frederick tells Werner that Werner's problem is that he still thinks he owns his own life. In the morning Werner wakes with a headache; he sees Frederick dressed and pointing out a small grey bird that has the ability to fly to Africa and back.

69: He Is Not Coming Back

Marie-Laure imagines she hears her father coming home, sitting next to her bed, but it is just the creaking of the house. After 20 days without him she will not get out of bed. She does not care that Etienne has been trying to get himself to leave the house the past few days; she no longer wants to go to the train station and ask the occupation authorities to find him, nor to beg Madame Manec to write a letter. She neither bathes nor eats, even though Madame Manec brings her delicious meals that she has pulled together from their rations. They receive a letter from the museum stating her father never arrived. Marie-Laure thinks of how he always said he would never leave her, and wonders why he did not come back. Everything in the house begins to scare her—the noises, the clutter, and the emptiness. Etienne tries to cheer her up by presenting science experiments. She overhears Madame Manec saying she is like a snail, curled up in her room. Marie-Laure is angry at everything and everyone.

70: Prisoner

The cadets are woken in the middle of the night and taken outside. There, volkheimer drags a thin prisoner in front of the group and ties him to a stake. It's February and very cold. Bastian tells them that the man escaped from a labor camp and tried to break into a farmhouse, and that he is an undersmenchen, worth nothing. Each boy must throw a bucket of water on the prisoner; the other boys cheer while they do it. The man slouches down and wrinkles the area between his eyes. Werner notes the growing uneasiness he has had since he was in Berlin. He has dreams of Frederick's mother as a demon, putting Hauptmann's triangles over her head. In this moment Werner tries to picture nice images from his childhood, but only ugly images appear—of the coal crane at pit number 9, and of the boy at training camp falling from the platform. He takes his turn and is glad it is over. When it's Frederick's turn he dumps the water on the ground. Bastian makes him try two more times, but Frederick refuses.

71: Plage du Mole

On the 29th day that Marie-Laure's father is gone, Madame Manec comes to her room and tells her to come downstairs to go outside with her, and to bring her cane. Madame Manec dresses her in a winter coat and they walk through the streets. It is early in the morning so there aren't many people out. They walk through a small gate and go down some stairs, and Marie-Laure realizes they are going down to the ocean. She is impressed by the scale of the ocean, the noise it makes, and how it's bigger than any body of water she has ever been near. She hears a man down there yelling, but it is just someone yelling to their dog. Marie-Laure is scared that the occupation authorities might stop them, but Madame Manec assures her they are doing nothing wrong. She takes off Marie's shoes and has her roll up her sleeves. Marie-Laure walks for hours, touching the sand, gathering shells and rocks, and wading in the water; then, finally, they return home. Marie-Laure goes to knock on Etienne's door, covered in sand. He says he was worried because they were gone so long. Marie-Laure hands him all of the objects she collected for him.

72: Lapidary

Von Rumpel is in Paris and has been staying at the Grand Hotel the last week. He has evaluated many other gems and specimens. He thinks back to the moment when he thought he held the Sea of Flames in his hand, and it felt so powerful he almost believed the myths. But soon he realized it was a reproduction: it had no inclusions, something that all real diamonds have. He went to work finding the person who made such a high quality reproduction, and found a half-Algerian man named DuPont. Von Rumpel enters DuPont's studio in the middle of the night and finds the evidence of the molds for the Sea of Flames. He has fake ration tickets given to DuPont so that DuPont is then arrested. Then, von Rumpel goes to visit him. DuPont is not in a jail cell: he is in an office with a secretary, handcuffed to a chair. DuPont appears to be physically fine, except for a crack in one of his glasses. Von rumple gets ready to question him.

Letter from Papa to Marie-Laure

In the letter, Daniel tells Marie-Laure that he has found an angel to deliver the letter to her. He tells her he is in Germany, and that the food they are giving him is unbelievably amazing. He tells her to be good to Madame Manec and Etienne.

73: Entropy

The prisoner is left outside frozen to the stake for a week. Boys go by to ask him directions, crows begin to sit on his shoulders, and eventually two 3rd-year boys and the custodian remove him. Frederick is chosen as the weakest 3 times in 9 days in their exercises; the commandant stands further away, counts faster, and Frederick is always caught and beaten. Werner does nothing to stop it or help him. Boys begin to put mice in Frederick's shoes and smear excrement on his field glasses. All Werner does to help is shine Frederick's boots and help him with his homework. In Dr. Hauptmann's lab, Werner has tested their first transmitter. In the lab, one day, Werner asks Volkheimer about the prisoner, saying it is not decent to have left him out there even after he was dead. Volkheimer said they do not care about decency, and that they do that to a prisoner every year. In technical sciences, Dr. Hauptmann asks the students what entropy is; Werner answers correctly that it is the degree of randomness or disorder in a system. Dr. Hauptmann says the Third Reich is trying to sort out the disorder in the system.

74: The Rounds

Etienne protests, but Madame Manec begins taking Marie-Laure to the ocean every morning. Soon Marie-Laure can lead the way there herself. She collects many shells and other objects, and loves to stick her hands and feet in the tidal pools near at the north end of the beach. Only there is she able to stop thinking about her father—whether what he said in his letter is a lie, why he is in prison, whether he will write again. Marie-Laure arranges her shells in order of species and size, and her room begins to smell of the ocean. After the ocean, Marie-Laure goes with Madame Manec on her errands, getting food and then delivering it to neighbors in need. Marie-Laure learns how much energy Madame Manec has, and how she is able to concoct full meals without many ingredients. She meets different characters of the city, including Crazy Hubert Bazin, a veteran from the Great War who sleeps in an alcove behind the library. He lost his nose, eye, and ear in the war, and wears a copper mask over half his face; he tells Marie-Laure stories of the city. March is Etienne's 60th birthday; Madame Manec makes clams and hard boiled eggs—the only two eggs she could find. Marie-Laure feels her life is more tolerable now, even though she misses papa. She examines the model of Saint-Malo, imagines all the characters she knows there, and then also imagines her father, outside of France, being offered platters of beautiful food.

75: Nadel im Heuhaufen

At midnight in the winter, Hauptmann takes Werner outside with his two dogs to test their transceiver. Volkheimer is somewhere in the area with the transmitter running, and using their two transceivers Werner has to figure out where Volkheimer is. Dr. Hauptmann drinks from his flask and appears giddy. Werner finds the transmitter signal and calculates the position of Volkheimer; he translates the position to the map, and they start out toward him, 2 kilometers away. As they make their way toward Volkheimer, Dr. Hauptmann talks of the moment as "sublimity": the moment when one thing is on the verge of becoming another. Werner wants to stop and check the position again; they are half a kilometer away. As they come over a hill, Dr. Hauptmann sees Volkheimer first, then Werner—he is lying face up in the snow, with the transmitter at his feet. Dr. Hauptmann pulls his pistol and tells Werner that this is the moment in which he should not hesitate. He aims at Volkheimer, and for a moment Werner believes he will shoot him, but he shoots in the air, the dogs go to greet Volkheimer, and the test was a success. While Dr. Hauptmann relieves himself, Werner does an impression of him, making Volkheimer laugh—he seems more like a child and less like a giant. Werner feels high the next day from the success.

76: Proposal

Marie-Laure listens in as Madame Manec's friends are gathered in her kitchen, discussing the issues they face with rations, and gossiping about other members of the town such as Big Claude and his wife, who are getting even fatter. Marie-Laure notes that they are giddy, whereas they should be serious and solemn. Madame Manec then deadbolts the door and reminds the women that they control a lot of the products and needs of the Germans in the city. The other women want to know what they'll be doing; she says it will not be anything extreme. After that exchange, some women leave, and six stay.

77: You Have Other Friends

The bullying of Frederick worsens: someone puts shit on his bed. Werner throws himself more into his work at the lab; they do two more tests that go even better and quicker than the first. Even with his success, he feels he is betraying something. Spring is coming, and one day as Volkheimer and Werner walk back from a test, Werner realizes Volkheimer will be sent soon to war. When Werner crawls into bed that night, he asks Frederick if he is awake, and then tells Frederick that maybe he should go home for a break, so when he comes back the boys might have forgotten about him. Frederick's reply is that they should maybe not be friends anymore. Werner says that is not what he meant.

78: Old Ladies' Resistance Club

Madame Manec and her friends begin a series of small resistances: changing the orientation of a sign so it points in the wrong direction; burning an important-looking letter from Berlin; putting goldenrod in a bouquet that is going to the Chateau when the officer there is allergic; and putting dog poop on the brothel steps. The old widow Madame Blanchard participates by neatly writing "Free France Now" on all of the five-franc notes. Madame Manec is giddy with scheming, and is surprised she can feel that way at 76 years old.

79: Diagnosis

Von Rumpel goes to the doctor to have his health checked. Von Rumpel thinks of the 19th-century Davenport he examined and had installed on a railcar that morning, and how the person showing it to him described how he got it by plundering a Chateau—though instead of 'plundering', he used the word "shopping." He thinks of other treasures he has seen lately, and imagines himself in the future walking through a Führermuseum full of these types of treasures, with the Sea of Flames in the middle. Von Rumpel is apparently one of the only Aryan diamond experts in the Third Reich, so he has a lot of responsibility. He has been examining fine art in addition to gems. The lapidary in Paris, Dupont, did not know any names, and made the Sea of Flames replicas out of a mold, stating he never saw the real thing. Von Rumpel now knows there are 3 fakes and one real, and he is looking to locate the remaining three stones. The doctor feels von Rumpel's groin and tells him he will need a biopsy.

80: Weakest (#3)

One morning Werner wakes and finds that Frederick is not in his bunk. He hears rumors of what might have happened to him: taken in the night by older boys, made to test his eyesight by shooting or by taking an exam. Werner feels all the stories have contradictions. He goes to the infirmary to check there, though to be caught skipping lunch would bring punishment. There he sees a bed covered in blood, and the nurse tells him the boy was sent to Leipzig for surgery. Werner asks when he will be back, and she shakes her head. He sits down and thinks of Jutta, and how he'll never be able to tell her about this.

Letter from M. LeBlanc to Marie-Laure

M. LeBlanc tells Marie-Laure the others in his cell are kind, that he is working on building a road, and that his "angel" is delivering the letter at great risk. He asks her, Etienne, and Madame Manec to keep sending him things, as it is possible a package may get through. He says he is safe.

81: Grotto

Marie-Laure and Madame Manec are with Crazy Hubert Bazin behind the library, and he asks to show them something. He leads them down some familiar streets, and then down a narrow alley. Madame Manec is anxious about where he is taking them. He unlocks a gate, and states they are underneath one of the granite walls. The floor in the narrow area slopes down toward water. Madame Manec declares it is gloomy, but Marie-Laure wants to see what is inside. Hubert shows her bunches of snails, a sea star, a dead crab, and mussels. He tells them that this area used to be a kennel for mastiff dogs that guarded the beach from soldiers, possibly as far back as 1165. The water is only ankle-deep in most parts. As a child, Hubert, Marie-Laure's grandfather Henri, and Etienne used to play here. When they leave, Hubert gives Marie-Laure the key.

82: Intoxicated

Frederick never comes back; he had a broken jaw and brain trauma. Werner sees his mother come and collect his duffle bag, Frederick's bed is filled with another cadet. The führer announces Operation Typhoon, the intention of taking over Russia. Volkheimer goes to war and there are rumors of him cutting off Russians' fingers and smoking them. Werner feels like all the cadets at Schulpforta are drunk, with the fervor that they throw themselves into their exercises and games. Werner misses Jutta and her sense of what is right, but he also resents her. Sisters are supposed to be sweet and rosy-cheeked, people you fight for. She writes him letters that are almost completely blacked out by the censor. He is only protected because he works for Hauptmann. The transceivers have begun to be sent out to be used and tested. In the lab Werner fixes the ones that come back broken. Hauptmann sometimes goes away for weeks at a time. Bastian tells the boys not to trust their minds, filled with questions, because they need clarity. Werner writes one short letter to Jutta stating he is fine. One night alone he tries to listen to the radio, to find the music Volkheimer used to listen to, but there is nothing but static.

83: The Blade and the Whelk

Marie-Laure and Madame Manec meet a man named Rene at the Hotel Dieu. Madame Manec says her name is Madame Walter and that Marie-Laure is her accomplice. Rene and Madame Manec talk, and Rene tells Madame Manec in a low voice what information is needed: the different types of license plates entering and leaving the city. Marie-Laure cannot hear all the info that is exchanged. She wonders if they pantomimed or exchanged notes. They go home and Madame Manec gets out the canning supplies—she has two rare boxes of peaches. As they can the peaches, Marie-Laure asks what a pseudonym is, and chooses one for herself: The Whelk. Madame Manec choose The Blade for herself. They laugh.

In between Chapters 83 and 84:

Werner receives a letter from Jutta that says she is working at the laundry with other girls where they mend clothing. People bring in all types of fabric to be used because of the shortage. Jutta sends Werner his old childhood notebook. The notebook is filled with his childhood questions and inventions. He feels an intense wave of homesickness.

84: Alive Before You Die

Madame Manec talks to Etienne about his joining in with her efforts. He expresses his fears of getting arrested; he worries that even opening the window will get him in trouble, but Madame Manec leaves it open. Etienne is worried about who can be trusted, and says that the only people who can be trusted are people with your same blood running through their veins. Marie-Laure listens in, and she realizes Madame Manec has been allowing Etienne's fears all his life. Madame Manec says Etienne can help by reading numbers into his old transmitter in the attic. They will get the numbers from Madame Ruelle, who will get them from Crazy Hubert and then bake them into her bread. He protests that no one will hear the transmissions, but Madame Manec says people do still have hidden receivers. She asks him if he wants to live a little before he dies. Marie-Laure listens outside the door. She thinks of how she used to ride on the back of her father's bicycle through Paris. Etienne says he needs to get back to his book.

85: No Out

In January 1942, Werner goes to Dr. Hauptmann and tells him he would like to go home. Dr. Hauptmann is surprised, especially because he has been giving Werner special treatment: he gets to eat chocolate and sit in the laboratory by the fire. Werner observes in Dr. Hauptmann something pitiless and inhuman. Dr. Hauptmann accuses Werner of believing he is something now, and reminds him he is an orphan with no family, that he can have him sent to the trenches to be fed to Russians. He directs him to come to the lab that night as usual, and informs him that the special treatment will stop. Werner imagines the moment of his father's death, being crushed in the mine, and realizes he wants to be neither here nor at home.

86: The Disappearance of Hubert Bazin

When Marie-Laure and Madame Manec go to deliver soup to Hubert, he is not there. The woman at the library does not know where he is, and he does not return. She calls a meeting with her group and only half the members attend. Some ask if Hubert was working delivering messages. They suggest maybe they should hold off for a while because it is getting dangerous. Marie-Laure wonders where they take people when they disappear—a Gasthaus like where her father is, perhaps? Some say they are sent to factories in Russia, or to camps in the mountains, or they just disappear. Every time she goes outside she feels the quiet there, unnatural, not knowing what might be watching.

87: Everything Poisoned

New silk banners appear in the cafeteria with nationalistic sayings; one talks of being slender. Werner finds worms in his sausage more than once. The electricity surges and goes out, the water in the showers is cold, and the instructors are called to war and replaced by townspeople with short tempers, many of them veterans from the Great War. Cars rarely come there, and food is delivered by a skinny mule. The two men who deliver news of dead fathers continue to come and tell cadets of their fathers' deaths; one cadet appears to be proud of his father for dying for his country. The commandant tells the cadets of what the führer needs: electricity and boot leather. However, Werner realizes that what the führer needs is boys, and men, to die in the war. In March 1942 Dr. Hauptmann calls Werner in his lab to tell him he has been called to Berlin.

88: Visitors

The bell rings while Etienne Marie-Laure and Madame Manec are having dinner. Two French policemen sent from the national museum are outside. One eats an apple. They sit at the table and refuse food. They say that they are not sure which German prison her father is at. They do not know if he is guilty, but he was accused of theft and surely was not given a trial. Although their French is perfect and they seem to be Frenchmen, Marie-Laure wonders if they can be trusted, because they are not family, as Etienne mentioned. They want to know if they can see the things Daniel Leblanc left behind. Etienne allows them to search the house. They look inside the big wardrobe on the 6th floor and they glance at the model of Saint-Malo in Marie's room. They warn Etienne for having 3 French flags rolled up, and he burns them after they leave. He tells Madame Manec that she can no longer have meetings in his house, and that she is forbidden from allowing Marie-Laure to participate with her.

Between Chapters 88 and 89:

Letter from Werner to Jutta, describing the lack of paper to write on, and the electricity outages. He says that Frederick was right; he goes to say what his problem is, but the rest of the letter is censored, except for the part saying, "I hope someday you can understand."

89: The Frog Cooks

Madame Manec treats Etienne and Marie-Laure coldly, like strangers. She still goes to the beach with Marie-Laure, but seems absent. She is out for much of the day. Marie-Laure and Etienne sit in the kitchen, and Etienne reads to Marie-Laure from a book on snails. The book says that snails can survive being in a block of ice, being dry in a matchbox for years, and can generate more shell material if their shells are damaged. Etienne exclaims that there is hope for him yet. He suggests that the two of them begin dinner because he does not think Madame Manec will come home. Neither of them does anything. Madame Manec returns and cooks potatoes; the tension in the room makes Marie-Laure dizzy. Madame Manec asks them if they know what happens if they put a frog in boiling water. She tells them: it jumps out; however, if a frog is put in cool water and then boiled, it gets cooked alive.

90: Orders

Werner is called to the office and told by the commandant's assistant that his age was recorded wrong: he is actually 18 years old, not 16 years old. Werner is aware that this is an absurd assertion, as he is still very small for his age. The man tells him that Dr. Hauptmann called their attention to this fact, and that Werner is needed in a technology division in Wehrmacht. The commandant had urged disciplinary action, but Dr. Hauptmann convinced them that Werner would be useful. The man hands him a helmet and tells him he will be given instructions in a fortnight.

91: Pneumonia

In spring, Madame Manec gets sick. The doctor prescribes rest aspirin and aromatic violet comfits. Madame Manec talks about how she is in charge of the world, that it is a big responsibility controlling every leaf that falls, every baby born. Etienne is a kind nurse, wrapping her in blankets; eventually, when she continues to shiver, he uses the rug to keep her warm.

Letter from Daniel LeBlanc to Marie-Laure: he tells her that he received her two packages, and that they would not let him keep the soap. He is now at posted at a cardboard factory. He reminds her of how there used to be two things on the table on her birthday, if she ever wishes to understand, he says, she should look inside Etienne's house. He says his angel is leaving, so he will try to get the letter to her.

92: Treatments

Von Rumpel receives treatment for his lymphoid tumors. The injections make him weak and dizzy, and also cause him to have confusion and trouble concentrating. In his hotel, wrapped in blankets, he unwraps a parcel that came from the Vienna library, where the librarian located a number of texts that contained information on the Sea of Flames—about the prince, and about the goddess who fell in love with a god. He closes his eyes and see a tongueless priest say "the keeper of the stone will live forever," and then he hears his father's voice tell him to see obstacles as opportunities.

93: Heaven

Madame Manec gets better for a few weeks and promises Etienne that she will stop her activities. Marie-Laure goes with Madame Manec on a walk to a market, and is certain that Madame Manec exchanged an envelope with a woman they passed on the way. They stop at Madame Manec's suggestion to lie down in a field of weeds, filled with the wildflower Queen Anne's lace. Marie-Laure listens to the bees and wonders how they know their role in things. Etienne taught Marie-Laure to distinguish insects by their sounds. She asks Madame Manec what she looks like; Madame Manec tells Marie-Laure she has thousands of brown freckles. They talk about what heaven is like and whether they will see God, even though Marie-Laure is blind. Etienne does not believe in heaven, but Marie-Laure wants to know if Madame Manec does. Madame Manec coughs. As the grasses and Queen Anne's lace sway around them, Madame Manec says she thinks heaven would be a lot like this.

94: Frederick

Werner spends the last of his money on a train ticket to Berlin, where he goes to visit Frederick. Berlin appears gloomy despite the sunshine. Before he goes in, he goes around the block twice. He rings Bell Number 2 and then realizes their name is now on Bell Number 5, where the Jewish woman Frau Schwartzenberger used to live. He goes up and Fanni opens the door. Then Werner's mother comes out, in tennis clothes, and, after a moment of reverie, greets him. She tells him Frederick will not recognize him, but to go in, and she leaves. Werner goes in and sees Frederick sitting at a table with a placemat in front of him, having apparently just been being fed. Fanni comes in and feeds him a few more bites, then cleans his face and clears the placemat. Frederick draws heavy spirals on paper. Werner asks Fanni for the bird book and looks around for it, but she insists they never had a book like that. Werner notes that the 5th-floor apartment is nicer than the 2nd floor. Werner tells Frederick he is going to the front. Frederick says to Werner, "You're pretty, mama." Werner listens to the stillness of the city, and thinks of all the birds Frederick used to know. He cannot bear to look into Frederick's stagnant gaze.

95: Relapse

Marie-Laure wakes in June 1942 and Madame Manec is not in the kitchen as she usually is. She knocks on her door, waits, and then enters. She hears Madame's rattling breath, smells sweat and urine, and when she touches her face she feels as if she is scalded. She runs to get Etienne. He calls in the doctors and Madame's friends, who all come over. Marie-Laure feels the first floor is too full; she paces the stairs. At 2 pm the doctor comes with a man who smells of dirt and clover who lifts Madame Manec and puts her on a horse cart, as though she were a bag of oats. Marie-Laure finds Etienne in the corner of the kitchen, whispering, "Madame is dead."

Analysis

Von Rumpel's cancer, which was briefly foreshadowed in Chapter 46, is diagnosed in Chapter 79, and discussed in its final stages in Chapter 62. His cancer is a metaphor for the darkness or evilness inside him. Even the imagery he uses when thinking of how his cancer—"A black vine that has grown branches through his legs and arms"—has an evil tone. Von Rumpel's dark intentions in finding the Sea of Flames, against all odds, have surfaced.

Motifs of vision and sight are explored as Werner, Volkheiemer, and Bernd are trapped in the dark cellar, with only Volkheimer's dying field light to illuminate their surroundings. Despite this, Werner begins to believe that he can see in the dark, a metaphor for his ability to see the good within himself despite the darkness or evilness of the Nazi party. Thus, Werner begins to link the former name of the cellar—in French, "atelier de reparation"—to his current emotional state of realizing he has been part of atrocities. The word "reparation," in addition to meaning "repairs" in French, can mean "reparations" or "atonement," which is apt for Werner's situation.

In Marie-Laure's narrative, she finds the only two remaining cans of food in the house; once again, survival occurs through family, love, and loyalty. This loyalty is also expressed through the utility of the alert system designed by Etienne to keep them safe: now, having the system is key to the survival of Marie-Laure. Meanwhile, Volkheimer is caring for the injured Bernd, and reminding Werner that life is worth living; the love and family loyalty he has developed for them thus also influences their survival.

As Part 5 begins, Werner goes to Berlin for the first time, experiencing the excitement of the city, as well as Frederick's rich lifestyle; the culture contrast for him is jarring, between what he has known and what he sees there. In Frederick's building, Werner meets the only Jewish person named in the book, Frau Schwartzenberger, who appears poor and timid in contrast to Frederick and his family's luxury lifestyle. Werner finds himself feeling uneasy about the attitude toward her. As Werner becomes more aware of his uneasiness surrounding the discrimination encouraged by the nationalist attitude that is worn proudly by Frederick's mother, Werner's first deep doubts about his choices begin to surface. But when Werner expresses his doubts to Frederick, Frederick tells him that his problem is that he still thinks he owns his life—thus, Frederick represents someone who has already been brainwashed past the point of doubting his participation in the Nazi regime.

In Chapter 70, the theme of cruelty of the name of nationalism is horrifyingly described. This chapter marks a more definite turning of Werner's awareness of the cruelty that the school is fostering in the boys. "We are a volley of bullets, sing the newest cadets, we are cannonballs. We are the tip of the sword" (Ch 82). Werner compares the state of the boys to intoxication, as if they were drunk or high on nationalism. As his doubts build, he thinks too of Jutta, and her opposition to his going there; at the same time, he also blames her for his not fitting in perfectly, and for his having these doubts. He that "Perhaps she's the impurity in him, the static in his signal that the bullies can sense."

Although Frederick said to Werner that they do not own their lives, in Chapter 70, it is Frederick who makes a choice by not throwing the water at the prisoner—one of the first examples of a humanist decision, starting the development of this theme where the characters have a choice in their own destiny and the destiny of other humans, meaning they can choose goodness. Sadly, Frederick's fate is determined by his action: later in the book, the phrase "What the war did to dreamers" arises as a direct reference to Frederick; because he made the humanist choice, he was tortured and beaten, and never was the same thereafter.

As the war progresses, the theme of science and technology becomes more complicated. While it was initially magical for Werner, at Schulpforta he sees how it is being used by the Third Reich for their purposes; as a demonstration of this, Werner dreams of an image of a demonic version of Frederick's mother putting Dr. Hauptmann's triangles over her head. The scientific concept of entropy also builds on the complicated theme of science and technology, as it crosses with the cruelty of German nationalism: Dr. Hauptmann says the Third Reich is trying to sort out the disorder in the system, the implication being that the non-Aryan people are that disorder. And yet, paradoxically, this entropy seems to be increasing, as Werner observes in Chapter 87: everything is poisoned, where they have limited electricity and food supplies, and many boys are losing their fathers in action.

"The time of the ostriches" is the title of Chapter 53; an extended metaphor implying that Etienne, Marie-Laure, and Madame Manec have had their heads in the sand while the world around them continues. As Marie-Laure deals with the disappearance of her father, she embodies the symbol of the whelk: Madame Manec says she is like a snail, curled up in her room. Marie-Laure recovers from the loss of her father only because of the family that has grown up around her. Formerly, her family was only her father; now it contains Madame Manec, Etienne, and the characters in the town she has begun to meet. Through this, she is able to discover the grotto, where she finds much peace among the snails.

As a way of pulling their heads of out the sand, Marie-Laure and Madame Manec find new life together, surviving the occupation by joining the French Resistance. Adding to the theme of nationalism, French nationalism contrasts with German nationalism. Marie-Laure wants her pseudonym to be the Whelk, a creature that is symbolic for Marie-Laure's resiliency and toughness. Although she is inside her shell—the shell being the house and her blindness—she is strong and determined.

As Madame Manec gains courage and strength in her nationalist resistance activities, she encourages Etienne to join. She asks him if he wants to live a little before he dies, which is an understatement: he has lived for many years, but has not experienced a lot of action in the past 20 years stuck inside his house. Madame Manec is trying to assist Etienne in his survival out of her loyalty to him. Later she uses the metaphor about the frog—put in boiling water it jumps out, but in a pot slowly being warmed and the frog cooks—to demonstrate to Etienne why he needs to participate in the resistance. Although Etienne later wonders whether this metaphor was meant to describe her or the Germans, the other possibility is that this metaphor describes himL he, doing nothing, in a pot slowly boiling, with slowly die, rather than fighting back against the occupation of his country.

Part 5 ends with Madame Manec's death. Now Marie-Laure has lost two of the parental figures in her life: her father and Madame Manec. Although she does not know at this point that she is the one carrying the Sea of Flames, the curse seems to be somehow affecting her still. In Werner's narrative, he is forced to join the Wehrmacht, and goes to tell his brain-damaged friend Frederick of his fate. Again, Doerr has effectively used the time structure of the book to create momentum between the narratives of the climax and the events leading up to it.

All the Light We Cannot See Chapters 96-120 (Part 6: 8 August 1944 - Part 7: August 1942) Summary and Analysis

Summary

Part 6: 8 August 1944

96: Someone in the House

Marie-Laure reasons that someone is in the house because she first heard the gate shut and then the door. She hears her father's voice in her head giving her bits of reasons: for example, the person is not Etienne because he would have called out to her. She feels distress and imagines herself a shell coiling into a shell. She imagines jumping out the window. Her father's voice tells her a rescuer would be calling out. She knows she has to hide. She has her cane, the cans, the knife, the brick, and the house with the stone in it. She recognizes the man's footsteps, an out-of-rhythm stride, a German sergeant major with a dead voice. Moving quietly, grateful she doesn't have her shoes, she goes into her grandfather's room and opens the wardrobe, where behind the doors Etienne has installed a false door. She goes inside, shuts the wardrobe doors, and then inches the false door shut. She asks the stone to protect her now, if that's what it does.

97: The Death of Walter Bernd

Bernd murmurs gibberish for an hour, then asks for light. Volkheimer feeds him the last of a canteen of water. Bernd tells the story of how he visited his father last year, who was very old. When he went to visit him his father told him he didn't have to stay, that he could go off with friends. Bernd left, even though he had come far to visit his father, and had no friends left to visit there. Not long after he tells this story, he dies. Werner works on making the radio work—perhaps not for Jutta, but rather so he doesn't have to think of Volkheimer burying Bernd in the rubble. Werner finds materials and a battery that they can use to keep the field light lit. He places the crushed transceiver on the table. He looks at the task as a problem to solve.

98: Sixth-floor Bedroom

Von Rumpel limps through the house, in and out of each room. He does not see any dollhouses. He worries he got everything wrong. On the 6th floor he sees Henri's neat room, then the small bathroom, and then Marie-Laure's room, full of seashells; there, he sees the model of the city, which is what he has been searching for. He thinks of how his daughters would love to see something like that. He has the sensation he has been here before, that he once had a room like this, as if the room had been waiting for his return. He believes the Sea of Flames will be inside the model.

99: Making the Radio

Werner wraps a wire around a pipe, and has connected the parts needed—ground, antenna, and battery. He raises an earphone to his ear, but the radio does not work. The hotel above them groans, then a shell explodes somewhere and dust falls on them. Werner envisions the distribution of the current; he rechecks all the parts, then tries again and finds the radio working. He remembers Jutta, and also thinks of Herr Seidler. He scans the channels and finds only static.

100: In the Attic

Marie-Laure hears the German shut the wardrobe doors, and she waits. She grows sleepy. She decides to climb up into the garret, where it is hot, the air trapped. She knows that the floors there are noisy, so she moves carefully. She wonders what she will do if the German comes in—hit him with the umbrella rack up there? She wants to open a can but knows she can't do it quietly. Outside she hears a shell flying. She is terrified. She wonders if he is gone but knows he is not, because she knows why he came here.

Part 7: August 1942

101: Prisoners

Werner meets an underweight corporal known as Neumann Two, who comes to greet him by foot. Neumann One is the driver, and there are an engineer and a sergeant as well. Neumann Two examines the uniforms that Werner brought, and is disappointed they are not in his size. They walk to the village, where Neumann Two orders calf livers at a delicatessen and eats them. He takes 3 pills for his back, and then asks for 12 hardboiled eggs to go, 4 of which he gives to Werner. They board a train in Schulpforta and ride until Lodz, where they get out on a platform full of sleeping soldiers, as if they were all enchanted, breathing in synchrony. They sit and wait, and after dark a train begins to pass: a locomotive, a few cars, a machine gun in a blister, and all the cars following are flatcars loaded with people, standing and kneeling. Neumann Two says they are prisoners. Each car seems to have sacks in a wall at the front to block the wind. Werner tries to see the individuals in the cars, and then suddenly realizes that the "sacks" are actually dead bodies, hundreds or thousands of men. Werner asks, "They were sitting on their dead?" Neumann Two responds by miming as if he were raising a rifle towards the train, and says, "bang."

102: The Wardrobe

Etienne does not come out of his study for days after Madame Manec dies. Madame Manec's friends bring food for Etienne and Marie-Laure, and take her to the memorial. After 4 days Etienne comes out of his room, comes to the kitchen, and asks the women to leave. Then he locks the doors, goes to the basement, and takes out an electric saw. They go to the 6th floor and saw a hole in the back of the wardrobe, then in the attic door. Etienne arranges the things in the attic. Marie-Laure falls asleep on her grandfather's bed. She wakes to music, Clair de Lune, and the recording of her grandfather. Etienne comes down stairs, and she knows what he will say. Etienne wants to participate in what Madame Manec is doing; he says that it is not a game, and he needs to know the routine. Marie-Laure says she will go to the bakery, and describes the way there. She will ask for bread, and Madame Ruelle will ask after Etienne, so as to be assured that Etienne is willing to participate. She will pay with a ration ticket. Then she will get the bread and come back. He tells her to go do it.

103: East

Werner and Neumann Two ride East, sleeping in the cars, watching thin pale soldiers get on and off. Occasionally they see an overturned, burnt train car. They arrive in Russia. They get off the train and walk through a charred village. Werner is brought to a captain eating a boiled round piece of gray meat. He asks Werner to look at the equipment. Neumann Two brings a lantern and shows Werner the back of a truck (an Opel Blitz), where the transceivers are, and leaves him there. Werner wonders whether this is Dr. Hauptmann's idea of punishment or reward. He thinks of Frau Elena and his sister, warm in front of the fire at Children's House. Werner feels soothed by the site of the transceivers, all the way out here like old friends. He opens the back and sees the damage. He remembers fixing Herr Seidler's Philco. As he opens the second transceiver case, Volkheimer appears.

104: One Ordinary Loaf

Etienne tears open the bread to find the paper string of numbers. He says they will wait until dark to read them. Etienne rigs the house with wires so they can tell if someone has entered the gate and front door: when this happens, bells go off on the third floor and in the attic. Marie-Laure tests the bells. Then Etienne builds a sliding false back on the wardrobe that can be opened from both sides. He puts the telescoping antenna in the chimney. He turns on the transmitter and reads the string of numbers on three frequencies, then turns it off. Marie-Laure asks what the numbers mean; he does not know. He asks Marie-Laure if she remembers what Madame Manec said about the boiling frog, and wonders if the frog was supposed to be her or the Germans.

105: Volkheimer

Werner meets the other people he is working with, and they tell him their captain believes that attacks of partisans hitting the trains are being organized by radio, Volkheimer assures them that Werner is better than their last technician. They take the Opel down the roads and stop every few miles to set up the transceivers. They leave Bernd and Neumann Two behind with a rifle and headphones, then drive further. Werner switches on the primary receiver, listening for unsanctioned sounds. At night they eat sardines, and Werner has nightmares of Frederick, and of Jutta staring at him accusingly. Volkheimer keeps checking to see if Werner has heard anything. In their tests, Werner always knew Volkheimer was out there transmitting, but now he is chasing ghosts. At night there is frost, and Werner wakes with his breath showing, wondering how deep will the snow be.

106: Fall

From the 5th floor of the house, Etienne watches German soldiers gathering for a photo shoot at the Bastion de Hollande, laughing in the wind. He sees three women leaving Big Claude's house, the only house on the block with electricity. He lights a candle and goes to the sixth floor. He has given up trying to crack the code of the paper. He has felt better since he has begun to read the paper on the radio daily: he hasn't struggled with his vision, nor with nausea. They have been reading the slips of paper for months, and now Etienne has also begun to play music. He imagines the people receiving the numbers do not expect the music. Tonight he plays Vivaldi. Marie-Laure comes to the attic, and they dance. He lets the music play too long, he thinks. He sees the glow on Marie-Laure's face, reminding him of dusks in places he used to go with his brother. The transmitter remains on after the song ends. After Marie-Laure goes to bed, Etienne sit by his own bed. He imagines the bony figure of Death riding the streets below, looking at the houses; he says to it, "Pass us by."

107: Sunflowers

Werner and his unit drive the Opel listening for the signals of foreigners. They are in a field of sunflowers, one transceiver in the truck; Bernd takes the other transceiver into the stalks to set up. Neumann One and Two talk about sex. Suddenly Werner hears Russian coming through the radio. He gives the coordinates to Bernd and they calculate the distance: 1.5 kilometers away. The truck takes off into the sunflowers, the stalks and heads hitting against the truck. Volkheimer distributes weapons; they see a cottage. They shut off the truck and Volkheimer, Neumann Two, and Bernd go on foot with their weapons. Werner listens to the radio, where a man continues to talk. He hears the shots first in the air and then on the radio. Volkheimer comes back with what seems like ink splashed on his face—then Werner realizes it is not ink. He tells Neuman One to burn the place, and Werner to salvage the equipment. Outside there is a dog that seems to be sleeping; inside are two dead men, and Werner notes they are not wearing uniforms. In the kitchen there are unlabeled potions in the cupboard, and one that says 'belladonna'. Werner takes their transmitter, a low-quality machine. Neumann One uses diesel to burn the place. Werner thinks of Dr. Hauptmann saying that a scientist is determined by his interests and his time; Werner thinks of all the events in his life that have lead him here, and watches the fire as they drive away.

108: Stones

Von Rumpel goes to a warehouse in Lodz, his first time traveling since he finished his treatment in Stuttgart. There, he is dressed in a jumpsuit and a Gefreiter (the officer in charge) explains the protocol: two other men, also in jumpsuits, will take the stones out of their settings, another man will clean them, and then von Rumpel will examine them and call out their level of clarity—included, slightly included, or almost loupe-clean. They will work in 12-hour shifts. They dump out a bag of jewels. Von Rumpel starts to ask where they came from, but then realizes he already knows.

109: Grotto

Marie-Laure still expects Madame Manec to come up the stairs in the mornings. When Marie-Laure wakes she always goes to the bakery via the same route, counting the storm drains. There she asks for an ordinary loaf, which sometimes contains a scroll and other times does not. Sometimes Madame Ruelle also gives her groceries. After she gets the bread she goes to the grotto, unlocks the door, and wades into the chilly water calf-deep. She observes all of the sea life there: a barnacle living inside a mussel shell; a hermit crab. That winter the electricity is off more than it is on, so they burn furniture and other things to stay warm. She takes the rug from Madame Manec's room to throw on top of her bed. She wonders if she should go stand in the front door while Etienne broadcasts, but stays in bed. She thinks of her father, dreams herself in the museum, and hears him say he'll never leave her in a million years.

110: Hunting

Werner continues to work on finding people transmitting from unpermitted transmitters. They find various locations and stop them. He feels successful. The captain promises them holiday leave and other treats. They drive through places that he and Jutta once recorded on their maps— places like Minsk and Prague. Sometimes when they are driving they pass prisoners in trucks and Volkheimer asks Neumann One to slow down. He looks for prisoners that are his size, of large stature, and when he sees one he gets out the the truck and orders the man to give him his clothes and his boots. The men comply but are always reluctant to give up their boots, knowing that without them they will die. Germans drive all over Russia; the roads are compacted ice and blood. In spring it begins to melt, but ice still remains.

One night Werner is in a restaurant a few tables away from a soldier who is reading with a surprised expression. Neumann One tells him that the reason the boy looks that way is because he lost his eyelids to frostbite. They are not able to receive mail, and Werner has not written to Jutta in months.

111: The Messages

Occupation authorities require that a list of the inhabitants of a house are posted on the door. In summer 1943 Madame Ruelle hands Marie-Laure another note in addition to the bread, a note that she wants Etienne to read. The note says that a monsieur wants his daughter to know he is alive and well. Marie-Laure and Etienne discuss what it means; Marie-Laure thinks it means exactly what it says. They continue to receive and read more messages like it—announcements, for example, of deaths and births. Etienne feels good knowing that ordinary people are listening to his broadcasts. He always reads the number, the messages, and plays a song, all on a few different frequencies. This is too long, Etienne thinks, but no Germans come for him. Each night Marie-Laure asks Etienne to read her the letters from her father. She asks him what he thinks her father meant when he said twice in his letter, "inside Etienne's house," but they've discussed it many times to no avail. Etienne thinks of the summer that he and his brother Henri tried to catch fireflies. After Marie-Laure falls asleep, Etienne hears a noise outside. He looks in the street and sees Madame Manec's ghost, collecting sparrows and putting them inside her coat.

112: Loudenvielle

Von Rumpel is in the Pyrenees. He waits to see the contents of a bag of gems taken from a man who was arrested. The man is affiliated with the National Museum. Von Rumpel still feels weak and queasy from his treatments. He sees a car pull up; a thin man with a black eye is taken out of the back, and a handbag is removed from the trunk. The captain and von Rumpel examine the contents: there are six felt pouches with gems, one of them a pear-shaped diamond. After examining it he knows it is a fake, but feels successful having found 2 fakes so far. He celebrates by eating a meal of wild boar and Bordeaux wine, a luxury.

113: Gray

December 1943 is very cold, and there is hardly any wood left to burn. Marie-Laure continues to deliver messages for Etienne to read. She can hear airplanes passing low overhead and fears some will crash into them, but none does, and nothing changes. The only thing that Marie-Laure notes has changed is that she has grown and cannot fit the clothes her father brought for her, nor her shoes: she wears Etienne's shoeswith three pairs of socks. There are rumors that all residents of Saint-Malo will be forced to leave except for essential personnel and people with medical reasons. Etienne says they will not leave. Marie-Laure spends parts of her days lost in memories of times when she could see the colors of the streets of Paris. Now her entire world seems gray, except in the moments when Etienne is broadcasting on the radio and playing the music—then she sees magenta, aquamarine, and gold for those five minutes.

114: Fever

Werner gets a fever with diarrhea, and all he can do is lie down in the back of the truck. His companions try to help; Neumann Two offers the pills he takes (which now Werner knows are not for backaches). It becomes 1944; he hasn't written to Jutta in a year. He continues to find illegal transmissions, and realizes that everyone really is a partisan: all non-Germans want the Germans out. The Russian partisans operate in an unsophisticated and disorganized manner, even though the resistance is said to be an organized, dangerous group. He thinks of Dr. Hauptmann's talk of entropy—that if it decreases in one system, it increases in another. To Werner, it appears they are all Hades. In February they are in the mountains, driving down switchbacks; Werner shivers in the back, Volkheimer covers him with a blanket. Out the window Werner sees, for a moment, Jutta in a cabin sitting at a table with Frau Elena and other children; next to the stove is a bin of dead infants.

115: The Third Stone

At a chateau in Amiens, outside of Paris, von Rumpel goes to check the contents of a safe. The home belongs to a retired paleontologist, and the chief of security took refuge there in the days after Paris was bombed. Inside the safe is a pear-shaped diamond. Von Rumpel hopes it is real, especially because his cancer has come back. He also knows that soon he will be sent into the war: all of the people out examining objects of value are soon going to be sent to fight. He wonders who the third courier of the Sea of Flames would be.

116: The Bridge

In a French village to the south of Saint-Malo, a German truck is blown up while crossing a bridge. Madame Ruelle whispers to Marie-Laure that there are rumors a resistance radio network helped facilitate this. The authorizes have blocked access to the rampart walkways and are in the process of blocking off the beach. Yet there is still a number inside the loaf. Etienne says he thought they would take a break. That night, part way into the song, Etienne abruptly stops the broadcast. He comes downstairs and tells Marie-Laure how many people died in the Great War. He says that what they are doing isn't just reading numbers. Marie-Laure responds by saying that they are the good guys—aren't they?

117: Rue des Patriarches

Von Rumpel goes to the building where Marie-Laure and her father used to live in Paris. He questions the landlady on the first floor, who is surrounded by cats. She says she receives a check mailed to her every month. Von Rumpel goes to the apartment and enters. Inside it's clear the occupants left in haste. He sees the string tied between two places, and the grip strips on the floor; then he finds a book in Braille and understands that the locksmith has a blind daughter, that he is a loyal employee of the museum, and thus he is the perfect candidate to carry the jewel. Von Rumpel sees the model of the neighborhood, the Latin quarter, and notices one house is more worn than the rest: the building he is in. He remembers the style of the safe that held the diamond at the museum, and notices some of the same details on the miniature house. Hoping there is something inside, he crushes it with his foot.

118: White City

Werner and the others arrive in Vienna. The town seems all white and empty. They drive around for a while; Werner can feel the fever still inside him. He wonders at the purpose of opera houses and other art when people are killing each other and the future seems so bleak. They stop in one place and Newman One gives them all haircuts. The narrator tells the reader that Newman One would have been a barber if he hasn't been scheduled to be killed in Normandy in 10 weeks. While they have their hair cut, they listen to waltz on the radio. Werner observes Volkheimer's softer side as he listens to the music, and contrasts that with the fact that he knows Volkheimer has killed over a hundred men. Werner observes a child in a maroon cape playing while her mother watches, and remembers the joy of playing on a spring day. He worries Neumann Two or Bernd will come and say something crass, but they don't, and Werner feels a little more hopeful. Later, he finds an forbidden broadcast on the radio; he traces it to a big apartment block where he sees an antenna outside. Volkheimer and Newman Two go up but don't find anything. Werner goes up 5 minutes later to check it out. He sees that what he thought was an antenna was a rod meant to be attach to a clothesline. He sits down on the unmade bed, observing smells and objects belonging to a woman. He looks at the wallpaper and his brain feels jumbled; the wallpaper seems to move. Then he observes the maroon, hooded cape hung on the doorknob; at the same time he hears a gargled scream from Newman Two, a shot, a woman's scream, and then another shot. He goes into the bedroom and sees the woman lying on the floor, and the little girl he saw earlier in the closet, with a surprised look on her face and a hole in her forehead. In his mind, he tries to will her to blink. He feels nauseous. They go back to the truck, and Werner is sick between his shoes.

119: *Twenty Thousand Leagues Under the Sea*

On Marie's sixteenth birthday, Etienne gives her the two-volume set of Jules Verne's *Twenty Thousand Leagues Under the Sea* in braille. It has been over 3 years since her father left, and 4 years since she read braille, but it comes back to her right away. She thanks Etienne and can't understand how he got it; he mentions the bookseller Monsieur Hébrard, and tells her she has made a lot of friends. She begins to read it aloud to Etienne, the story coming back to her: the question of whether the creature seen is a reef or a sea monster; Professor Aronnax going to check it out, and then finding himself on Captain Nemo's submarine, the *Nautilus*.

120: Telegram

A new garrison commander arrives on the emerald coast. Even though he is of shorter stature and is prematurely gray, he gives off the impression that he is tall and powerful. He came with a French secretary. He is based in Saint-Malo, where he sends off telegrams nightly. In April 1944 he sends off a telegram that alerts Europe that there is a terrorist radio transmission coming from the area in or near Saint-Malo.

Analysis

In Part 6, Marie-Laure calls on her father, in her imagination and her memory of him, to help her survive being in the house with von Rumpel. Werner begins to put together the radio, thinking of it as a problem to solve. His survival up until this point has depended exactly on his skill of fixing radios.

In Part 7, both Werner and Marie-Laure are getting to work in their respective situations of participating in nationalism for their own country. Werner joins the Wehrmacht, where for the first time he is exposed to the atrocities the Germans are committing against others. Yet, there with his new unit, amongst the radio, he feels comforted and thinks of family—of Jutta and Frau Elena. He has a contrast of the truth of the atrocities the Germans are committing, and his own survival in what he has made important to him: working with radios, and using his skills in science and technology. Werner feels successful in that he is able to accomplish the task that is assigned to him—finding the partisan broadcasts—but the success is a lot bloodier than he imagined. He has nightmares where he sees Frederick and Jutta: both of them have made ethical decisions to respect human life, and they stand accusing Werner. He is also somewhat disturbed by how the Partisan broadcasters are not very threatening: they are poor and don't have good equipment. One of the most powerful images is when they are driving through the sunflowers and come upon a pretty cottage; this pleasant country imagery is juxtaposed with the violent act that they are committing. Werner complies with all the actions required of him, but his doubts are still in his mind. As Werner spends more time with his unit completing his tasks, he gets more and more isolated from Jutta—not writing with her, and thus straying farther away from the humanism she encompasses. Werner also becomes physically sick, a physical reflection of the spiritual and emotional hardships he faces while carrying out his gruesome tasks.

Meanwhile, Marie-Laure and Etienne are invigorated by their participation in the French Resistance. Marie-Laure spends more time amongst the snails and other creatures in the grotto, which is Marie-Laure's symbolic shell. In Chapter 111 the theme of memory appears as the viewpoint changes for a chapter to Etienne. The imagery of Etienne's mind is revealed to the reader in this part, as we see the hallucinations he has—of death walking the streets, and of Madame Manec's ghost on the street. Etienne's memories of his brother and himself as a child also come to him, strengthening him for the task of participating in the resistance. Etienne and Marie-Laure are even more surprised that there are others out there who want to share family news via the radio—births and deaths—also highlighting the theme that family love is what helps the characters to survive.

In one of the only moments of doubt for Etienne since he agreed to join the resistance, he expresses concerns that his broadcasts are leading to deaths, a concern that he relates back to the horrors he saw in the Great War. His words echo Dr. Hauptmann's words to Werner in Chapter 58: he said "it's only numbers" to reassure Werner that he was completing his job as necessary, and that he should not worry about the consequences. However, Etienne's perspective is the humanist one, as shown when he says, "These numbers, they're more than numbers." Etienne believes in the goodness of humans, that they have a choice not to harm each other; thus he questions if what he is doing is right.

In Part 7, as von Rumpel's cancer worsens, he begins to believe in the power of the stone, and wants to find it more for that reason than any other. In addition, he knows he will be sent to war soon, building on the growing evidence of the Germans losing the war. This mood is portrayed through the imagery from the German side of the war, showing their disorganization and lack of resources. When seen from Werner's point of view, the narrative takes on a bleak tone: Volkheimer stealing clothes off prisoners the same size as him; the Neumann's stealing weapons and clothes off dead partisans; the ice and blood paving the roads. Also, there is an allusion to Greek literature in "the White City" of Vienna, where Werner thinks of Hades: he feels the places he visited are like the Greek conception of Hell and the Underworld. He thinks of the theory of entropy discussed by Hauptmann but is not convinced any longer of its truth: it does not seem to be true for Germany and the Third Reich, because everything he sees is in disorder.

Chapter 118 is one of the most jarring and emotionally intense chapters of the book, in which Werner and his unit murder a mother and her young daughter accidentally. The chapter is rich with imagery and themes. It starts with the unit pulling into the seemingly empty city of Vienna, and stopping to get haircuts from Neumann One. In a paragraph of exposition, the author ironically describes what Neuman's life would be like as a barber, if he were not set to die in 10 weeks. Werner chooses music to play on the radio that Volkheimer would like, to please and support him in a time when the rest of the mood is bleak. At the same time, Werner is also reflecting on Volkheimer's actions as part of this unit, how he has been killing many people, and contrasts that with his soft side; the humanist in Werner still sees the good in Volkheimer, the Volkheimer who likes classical music. Werner is uplifted when he watches the little girl in the hooded cape play; ironically, this girl is the same one senselessly murdered by Neumann Two when Werner miscalculates the location of an illegal radio.

Part 7 ends with a telegram from the Germans alerting the surrounding areas of the resistance broadcast; thus, Etienne and Marie-Laure are endangered, and once again the momentum of the time switching in the novel is maintained.

All the Light We Cannot See Chapters 121-147 (Part 8: 9 August 1944 & Part 9: May 1944) Summary and Analysis

Summary

Part 8: 9 August 1944

121: Fort National

On the third afternoon of the siege of Saint-Malo, there is a lull in the shelling. Some horses kick through a garage door and run in the streets. Around 4 pm an American Field howitzer misfires a shell to Fort National where 80 Frenchmen are imprisoned, killing 9 instantly.

122: In the Attic

Marie-Laure isn't sure how much time has passed in the attic, but she is starving. She reasons with the voice of her father in her head: the German has left, and she can open the cans, which will make noise. However, her father's voice tells her that she didn't hear the bells go off, and the German would not leave without what he came to get. She hears the German using the toilet downstairs and exclaiming something in German, sounding as if he is in pain. She hears the creaking of her bed, and she wonders if he was sleeping there. She considers biting her arm to drink the liquid there. Finally shells begin to fly, making loud noises. During these noises she gradually opens one can. She peels the lid up and drinks; it is beans, and she eats the whole thing.

123: The Heads

Werner cannot locate any signal, only static on the radio. The battery is almost dead. They also have the extra battery Werner found to power the radio or the field light. They are out of food and water. In the corner of the basement there are white statues of heads that seem to emit a whiteness even in the dark. Werner crawls over to his friend Volkheimer and asks him if he ever heard the stories the boys at Schulpforta told about him. He said yes, and that he didn't like being asked how tall he was all the time. Werner wants to know if the grenades would work to get them out, but Volkheimer says they'd be crushed. There is enough battery to either run the transceiver another day, or to run the light. But they don't need light to use the rifle.

124: Delirium

Von Rumpel is in the bed, soaked in sweat, the taste of blood in his mouth. Ash blows in the window. He wonders if it is dawn. He looks at the model again. He has searched every inch of it, but the only house he needs, the model of rue Vauborel Number 4, is missing. He wonders if the girl took it with her when she left with Claude Levitte. However, he suspects the Sea of Flames is in the house, because the house still stands while others nearby crumble. Also, the old man did not have the stone on him when he was arrested and taken to Fort National—von Rumpel made sure of it. Von Rumpel tells himself he needs to get up again and look, starting in the kitchen.

125: Water

It begins to rain. Marie-Laure thinks this is good because it will put out fires. She hears the German go downstairs and wonders if this is an opportunity to go get water from the buckets she filled and put outside her room. She brings the empty can to fill that too. She waits for her father's voice to protest, but it does not. She goes to the attic door and listens. She thinks that maybe the German went down noisily but quietly came back up and will shoot her. When she exits the wardrobe, no shots come. In her mind, she summons the childhood image of her grandfather who takes one of her hands, and Etienne takes the other. She imagines what the house must have been like when they were boys. In her room she smells an odor left by the German, a smell of vanilla with something putrid underneath. She goes and finds the bucket, drinks fully from it, and then fills her can. As she turns to go back she hears him downstairs, 3 or 4 floors down, ransacking a room. As she finds the doorway, she finds her braille book on the floor; the German must have thrown it off her bed. She thinks about trying to sneak down to leave, but she does not want to die. She carries the book with her, climbs back inside the wardrobe, and shuts the door.

126: The Beams

In the dark of the cellar, Volkheimer begins to talk of his great grandfather. Volkheimer is standing, crouching under the low ceiling, portrayed like Atlas with the weight of the world on his shoulders. He says his grandfather was a sawyer. Ships back then had sails and needed masts, but there were no trees big enough, so they took them from the forests of Prussia, where Volkheimer grew up. He says his grandfather told him they would put wedges in the trees and sometimes it would take days for them to fall, and Volkheimer would imagine horses pulling the trees across Europe to be given a new life as masts. Werner thinks of the professor who said coal is a tree that is millions of years old, and says that, where he grew up, they dug up old trees. They both say they were desperate to get out. Shells continue to shake the cellar. Werner thinks of Jutta.

127: The Transmitter

Marie-Laure locates the transmitter on the table in the attic. She thinks maybe someone still has a radio—maybe the Americans, or others in the resistance, or even Germans in their hideouts. She raises the antenna; it makes a noise. She waits to see if the noise has alerted the German in her home. She turns on the transmitter and the microphone. She worries the thrum of the transmitter is too loud, but her father's voice tells her it is like the breeze. Being blind is different than just shutting her eyes. She is in another older world. She hears miles away, families moving in cellars, flies landing on corpses; she feels the land Saint-Malo rests on, hears the bones of a dead whale at the bottom of the sea, its marrow feeding millions of creatures that never see light. She thinks of how she said she would read to Etienne. She opens the book and brings the microphone to her mouth.

128: Voice

Werner hears a girl's voice speaking crisp French. At first he thinks he is hallucinating, but he wants to hear more. He thinks of himself in his bunk in Children's House, with Jutta trying to wake him out of a dream. The girl continues a narration about being submitted in water and stuck between two large pieces of ice. Suddenly she hisses, "he is here, he is right below me," and then it cuts out. Werner goes over to Volkheimer and tells him, trying to get him up, but he won't move. He tells Werner it's no use. They are both starving and weak. He thinks of the girl; he wants to save her. The chapter ends on a metaphor: god is a white cold eye watching the city being pounded to dust.

Part 9: May 1944

129: Edge of the World

Werner rides in the back of the truck, curled up under a bench. Volkheimer reads him a letter Jutta wrote, telling him that Herr Seidler has heard of his success and sends his congratulations, that Frau Elana's toothache is better, and also that she has started to smoke. Werner sees the dead redheaded girl in the cape floating, following them. Werner thinks of how someone at Schulpforta once told him about a rally for the führer, at which he spoke and there was a feeling of righteousness in the crowd. The only one who doubted that feeling was Jutta. They drive into France and stop and eat. He sees the dead girl's image in the flowers, and then it disappears. They continue driving until they reach Brittany. When they stop Werner gets out and goes to the beach, crossing a bunch of barriers. He sticks his hand in the water and tastes the salt. He hears people yelling, looks up, and sees a bunch of people watching him; he goes back to the town and his companions tell him the beach is full of mines. They go see the Kreiskommandantur, who tells them there is a radio announcement every night with numbers, then birth and death announcements, then music. They don't know what it means.

130: Numbers

Von Rumpel visits a doctor who tells him he only has 3 or 4 months left to live. He has a tumor in his throat and in his small intestines. He then goes to a dinner party where other officers talk of the retreats and the number of their men who have died—10,000. Liver is served, and von Rumpel doesn't eat it. He gets a call from France at the restaurant, from a man named Jean Brignon who has information on Daniel Leblanc, the locksmith from the national museum. Jean Brignon wants von Rumpel to help his cousin in exchange. Von Rumpel does not remember Jean, but he solicits the information nonetheless: the information is that Daniel Leblanc was arrested for conspiracy because they found measurements he made of Saint-Malo. The tip that lead to his arrest was from Claude Levitte. He does not know which camp Leblanc is in. He asks von Rumpel to help his cousin, but von Rumpel hangs up.

131: May

May 1944 feels heavy and humid to Marie-Laure, much like the May of 1940 before she left Paris. Plants are in bloom. Marie-Laure goes to get the bread, and Madame Ruelle reaches across the counter and holds Marie-Laure's face, saying, "you amazing child." She tells Marie-Laure to tell her uncle that the hour has come. The mermaids have bleached hair. They'll be coming within a week. She says it is a wonderful day. She gives Marie-Laure a large loaf of bread and a huge head of cabbage. Marie-Laure knows Etienne has heard on the radio that the British are putting together an armada of boats, including any boat available to join their fleet. After getting the bread, Marie-Laure goes to the grotto; the beach has been blocked off for weeks because of the mines. In the grotto, however, she can still sit with her snails and sea creatures, dream she is in Captain Nemo's submarine, and remember what it was like to be with her father.

132: Hunting (Again)

Werner and the others spend weeks driving around looking for a signal. Werner and Bernd are given a hotel room in the top of an old requisitioned hotel. At night Werner knows the dead girl from Vienna walks the halls, hunting for him. Werner stands in the hexagonal tub in the top floor of the hotel, and above him a 9-foot-long queen bee is on the ceiling.

Werner writes Jutta a letter. He tells her the fever is mostly gone. He describes how he loves the sea, how he sees so many colors in it, and how it seems to contain everything anyone could every feel. He sends his best wishes for Frau Elena and the children.

133: "Clair de Lune"

Werner's team is working a section of the old city of Saint-Malo tonight. It is raining. He has been listening in on his transceiver; Bernd is on the other one on a parapet under a poncho, but he has not touched his handset in hours, meaning he is sleeping. Suddenly he hears a voice announcing family news, then saying what time the next broadcast is—Thursday at 23:00—followed by music. Werner feels a memory coming at him of the same tenor of voice, the same quality of the transmission of the French Professor to whom he and Jutta used to listen. He feels as if he has been drowning for so long, and someone has suddenly brought him up for air. Werner observes the others: Volkheimer is sleeping on the bench next to him, and the Neumanns are asleep in the front. He waits for Bernd to say he heard something, but he does not say anything. The piano music is familiar; Werner recalls Jutta leaning toward him, Frau Elena in the background kneading bread. No one else heard. Werner thinks of how Frederick told him they didn't have choices and they don't own their lives, but in the end it was Frederick who *did* make a choice: the choice to not dump the water out on the prisoner. It was Werner who did not make choices. Werner goes to leave the van, and Volkheimer asks, "Nichts?" Werner confirms: nothing to report.

134: Antenna

An Austrian Air lieutenant sets up his detachment at the Hotel of Bees, taking apart the 4th floor and installing a cannon on the ramparts. Werner knows he is committing treason by lying and saying he heard nothing, but when he thinks of the piano music, he is filled with happiness. He also thinks of all the men dying in Normandy, and how in Saint-Malo all is still held by the Germans. Phrases the Frenchman used to say would come back to him, such as " So how, children, does the brain, which lives without a spark of light, build for us a world of light?" Werner knows the antenna must be very high because it used to reach him all the way in Zollverein, and he realizes the man must be using a chimney. Werner is worried that Volkheimer already suspects something is amiss, but he still goes out on foot on Thursday at the time of the broadcast. He walks through the streets and sees the antenna rise from one of the chimneys, on a high house on the edge of the sea, rue Vauborel Number 4. He hears in his head the Frenchman, "Open your eyes and see what you can with them before they close forever."

135: Big Claude

Von Rumpel goes to visit Big Claude to get information on Daniel LeBlanc and where he lived. To travel to Saint-Malo, von Rumpel has made his way through Breton on false pretenses of finding paintings in old summer homes, sometimes paintings he knows do not exist. Big Claude is not very forthcoming with information, his eyes seeming to say, "Give me." However, when von Rumpel turns to walk out, Claude reveals where Daniel LeBlanc lived: in Number 4 rue Vauborel.

136: Boulangerie

One day later, Werner is able to go back to the house on a misty morning. He fantasizes that he will ring the bell and be invited in to talk about the broadcasts and about science, but he knows that if he rings the bell the man will think he is being arrested. Werner sees a girl exit the house; she is pretty, with auburn hair and freckles. He worries she saw him staring, until he realizes she is blind. She wears ripped stockings, shoes that are too big, and a stained skirt. He watches her use her cane to find all the storm drains, and he follows her to the boulangerie. Outside the boulangerie Werner observes his surroundings, and sees across from him a sallow and goitrous sergeant major reading a newspaper. Werner wonders why he is shaking. The girl steps out of the boulangerie with her bread, counting under her breath. Werner is riveted, and she walks on into the fog.

137: Grotto

An American plane is shot down and the pilot climbs to shore, only to be taken prisoner. Etienne sees it as a tragedy. Madame Ruelle sees it as exciting, saying he is movie-star handsome. Marie-Laure has continued to read Jules Verne to Etienne; they have begun Volume 2. Today Marie-Laure takes her load and goes down to the grotto, touching the snails and anemones inside. When she comes out, a voice asks her what is inside, and what she has in her bag. The voice is speaking French, but she knows he is German. She says she was collecting snails, but he observes she has none. She worries about the loaf in her bag that probably has a scroll inside. She asks if she can pass, and he asks her if he can ask her about her father. She tries to act as if her father will come, but the man knows her father is in prison. He comes at her and slips; she goes inside the grotto, shuts the door, and locks it. He waits outside. He paces and tells her he has one simple question, after which he will leave. She curls into herself and imagines she is a whelk, impervious.

138: Agoraphobia

Etienne counts the minutes that Marie-Laure has been gone. It usually takes her 21 minutes, one time 23. This time it has been 31. He knows it takes 4 minutes to walk to the bakery and 4 back; he does not know where she goes in between but he suspects it is the sea, because she comes back smelling of sea water. He trusts she keeps herself safe. The last time Etienne went outside was 24 years ago. He thinks of that time, when he tried to act normal but felt his feet pounding and eyes in the cobblestones and corpses in the shadows; afterwards, he came back and crawled into bed. Now he feels a terrible headache coming on. He braces himself, and steps out the door.

139: Nothing

Marie-Laure waits inside the grotto while the German runs his newspaper over the bars. He wants to know what her father was doing here between June and January when he was arrested, and if her father left her anything. Marie-Laure breaks open the bread and eats the paper inside. The snails at her feet rasp away at the floor, with their 80 rows of 30 teeth. The sergeant major shares that he has been sent on pointless tasks, but all he really wants to find is this one thing. He said if she answers him he'll leave and not tell anyone about this place, God's promise. She thinks about what "God's promise" means. Marie-Laure finally answers him, that her father left her nothing: just a broken promise and a dumb model of the city. She is surprised by her anger. The German is quiet, perhaps considering her exasperation. She asks him to keep his promise and leave.

140: Forty Minutes

Etienne feels assaulted by the sun as he makes his way to the bakery. Madame Ruelle is surprised to see him; he tells her that Marie-Laure has not come back and it has been 41 minutes. He struggles with the sunshine. He tells her that sometimes Marie-Laure goes to the sea, and she says that's not possible with the beaches and the ramparts closed. Madame Ruelle is worried they will find the bread. Etienne suddenly remembers the old kennel where he used to play with his brother and Hubert. He and Madame Ruelle run through the streets and arrive there, where they see Marie-Laure crouched with bread broken in her lap. She lets them both in, and is surprised and relieved that they came.

141: The Girl

The blind girl haunts Werner. He thinks of her fearless step. They continue to search for the resistance signals. The blind girl faces down the dead Viennese girl inside him. He wants to know who she is. He is concerned that Volkheimer and the others already suspect that he knows something. He and Jutta used to pray that their whole world would freeze over, that they would wake up and find everything gone. He wishcs for that now. In August, Neuman One and Two are taken to the front—all essential men are needed for the defense. Neumann Two leaves looking as though he is in his last hours on earth. Only Volkheimer, Bernd, and Werner remain. That night, Werner decides that at the time of the broadcast he will either turn off the transceiver or cover the meter.

142: Little House

Etienne tells Marie-Laure he will get the bread now, and that he should have been doing it all along; Marie-Laure is relieved. She has nightmares of the German. They do not have much to eat in the house. Marie-Laure thinks of how the policemen 2 years ago asked her if there was anything specific her father mentioned, and how the German wanted to know if her father left anything with her. On the 6th of August, Marie-Laure reads to Etienne from Jules Verne, a passage about how Professor Arronnax wonders if Captain Nemo is carrying out a secret mission unknown to him. Marie-Laure closes the book and tells Etienne she needs to rest. She thinks of the letter she received from her father about looking inside Etienne's house. She realizes the German is not after the transmitter. She goes to her room and feels the model house of Number 4 rue Vauborel. She presses in a recess at the door and releases it, then shakes it, but hears nothing. Still, she easily solves the puzzle, twisting the chimney, sliding off the roof panels, and turning over the house, which drops a pear-shaped stone into her hand.

143: Numbers

The Americans seem to be winning: Etienne hears that liberation is a matter of days away. At the bakery Madame Ruelle unlocks the door and lets him in, telling him they need the coordinates for flak batteries. He says he will need to take measurements with a compass, but she says it is vital. Also, tomorrow, there is talk that all men ages 18-60 will be imprisoned in case they are part of the resistance. Etienne feels he is being caught in spiderwebs, but he nods and agrees to the plan.

144: Sea of Flames

Marie-Laure picks up the stone repeatedly, and sets it down as if it burns her. She thinks of how Dr. Geffard told her how queens may have worn it. She realizes this stone is what the German wants. She thinks about throwing it in the sea. She realizes it must be real if her father went through so much to conceal it. She considers showing it to her uncle. She thinks of her museum tour and how a boy on it asked, "When was the last time you saw someone throw five Eiffel Towers into the sea?" She tells herself curses are not real, and then she puts the house back in the model.

Early the next morning, Etienne knocks on her door and says he is going out. She asks him where, and he says it is better if she doesn't know. She asks what will happen when they bomb, and if they will hit houses; he says they won't. He says he'll be back when she wakes, and then they will finish the book together. She asks Etienne if he is ever sorry she came, and if she seems to be a curse; he says she is the best thing that has ever come into his life.

145: The Arrest of Etienne LeBlanc

Etienne feels good when he leaves the house. He already was able to transmit the location of the cannon beside the Hotel of Bees. He will choose two known points and calculate the 3rd to find the battery. It's pre-dawn, and no one is up and about in the city. He has the sensation that he is walking down the aisle of a train with all the other passengers sleeping. Then, he turns a corner and a man limps toward him out of the blackness.

146: 7 August 1944

When Marie-Laure awakes, Etienne is not there. She tries not to panic. She eats a piece of bread and fills two buckets of water, as well as the bathtub on the 3rd floor. She opens her book and counts 9 chapters left; she doesn't want to finish without Etienne. She checks that the little house is still under her pillow. She tries to read a chapter earlier in the novel. In the afternoon she hears the tripwire go off, but it is not Etienne—it is Claude Levitte. She opens the door halfway; he tells her Etienne told him to get her to take her out of the city, because of the evacuation orders. She doesn't believe that he talked to Etienne; her uncle wouldn't have asked Claude to escort her to shelter. She insists on staying. She thinks someone put Claude up to this. She closes the door and locks it.

147: Leaflets

In the Hotel of Bees, the Austrians serve pork kidneys on china plates with a silver bee etched in the rim. After dinner, Werner stands in the hexagonal tub on the top floor and looks out the window, observing that the Americans have them pinned against the sea. Orders have been posted by the garrison commander that no one should attempt to leave the city. Right before Werner closes the shutter, a plane flies over and drops leaflets, in French, that say, "Urgent message to inhabitants of this town. Depart immediately to open country."

Analysis

Trapped in the cellar, Volkheimer stands hunched under the weight of the ruins above him; Werner thinks of him as Atlas in an allusion to Greek mythology. Volkheimer holding the world on his shoulders is a metaphor for the guilt he carries in his actions in the war. Werner sees the heads emitting a white light in the attic, evoking the motif of vision and sight, and the theme of darkness and light. Here Werner is able to see in the dark, meaning perhaps he will also be able to see his own goodness in the darkness. Volkheimer shares a memory of his grandfather with Werner, of how they harvested trees; Werner, in contrast and an inverse parallel, realizes he came from a place that harvested trees that had been dead for millions of years.

Marie-Laure uses her imagination, combined with the strength she draws from family love, to find courage as she has to venture out of the attic in order to drink water. She conjures, in her imagination, the image of her grandfather, and of Etienne, to lead her safely to the buckets of water. Back in the attic, she calls on her father to help her with the radio broadcast, too, and she hears his reasonable voice in her head, telling her what noises are too much and what she can do safely, thus helping her survive unnoticed by von Rumpel downstairs. Unlike the resistance broadcasts, the reason Marie-Laure wants to use the transmitter isn't related to nationalism; rather, it is related to humanism: she is hoping her voice will reach someone in need of hearing something during this terrible event.

Chapter 121 tells of the accidental shelling of Fort National, where we know Etienne is currently being held—however, we don't know whether he is safe or not. Again, the idea of the curse runs through the narrative. Is the curse causing Marie-Laure's bad luck: is she unlucky enough to lose Etienne in addition to those she has already lost?

Chapter 127 is exposition of Marie-Laure's supernatural ability to hear and feel things that are miles away. The supernatural abilities of Marie-Laure are part of the fairy-tale nature of this story: a girl who can see more than anyone but is blind; a stone that can save one person but hurt all they love. Ironically, the supernatural element of the story is a sharp contrast to the humanism theme, because humanism rejects the idea of any supernatural or religious elements controlling human behavior: rather, it is humans who have the choice to do good or bad. This is apparent in the ending of Part 8 in the metaphor, "God is a white cold eye watching the city be pounded to dust." Thus it is human choice that holds the most power in the novel, despite the fairytale imagery: in things both good and bad, humans are what creates the movement of the novel's plot.

In Part 9, as the plot builds to the climax, Werner and his unit arrive in Saint-Malo and are told of the broadcast that lists numbers, reports family news, and plays music. The German officials are puzzled by it because they do not understand the music. Ironically, it is the music in the end that saves Etienne and Marie-Laure, because the music is what makes Werner sure he has found the same broadcast he used to listen to as a child. Werner's discovery of the broadcast is described with two powerful similes. In the first, the voice of Etienne hits him as if it were a six-car train coming out of the darkness at him—the darkness here symbolizing the evilness which has surrounded Werner. The other Werner feels "as if he has been drowning for as long as he can remember and somebody has fetched him up for air" (Ch 133). Breathing again, seeing again, Werner is finally ready to make choices that concord with the kindness inside of him, instead of with the twisted nationalism he has been participating in.

As the date of the bombing approaches, Marie-Laure parallels the heaviness of summer in Saint-Malo in period that lead to the bombing of Paris. Marie-Laure has the ability to see grayness, colors, and the coming of something dark.

As the British near and the geopolitical conflict builds, so does the conflict build for von Rumpel as he comes closer to finding the diamond and pursues Marie-Laure, who locks herself in the kennel. In there, she thinks of herself as a whelk, "impervious"—once again the symbol of the whelk appears as a strong steady creature. This strong, steady creature is up against von Rumpel, who is also known for his patience; Marie-Laure wins this round simply because she is not yet aware that she is the one who holds the Sea of Flames.

Marie-Laure finally discovers the location of the Sea of Flames; ironically, she only discovers it after her encounter with von Rumpel, because of the way he convinced her father left her something. In addition, she makes the discovery after reading a line in the Jules Verne novel about how Captain Nemo seemed to have some secret mission he was on that no one else knew about: suddenly, Marie-Laure thinks of her father, and the words of the letter he wrote; the reader can recall the anxious energy Daniel LeBlanc had when he arrived in Saint-Malo, the way he constructed to model of Saint-Malo as if he were on a deadline. All of it parallels the time when Marie-Laure used to solve puzzles for fun with her father; this time, the puzzle is more complicated and has a more valuable and dangerous reward: the Sea of Flames. At the same time, upon discovering the diamond, Marie-Laure begins to wonder if she has brought a curse on her family and those around her, and asks Etienne about this. However, in Etienne's eyes, Marie-Laure's arrival opened his eyes, helping him to live again: her arrival assisted in his survival through familial connection and loyalty, and so he does not see her presence as a curse.

The novel began in medias res, when the leaflets fell from the sky advising the inhabitants of Saint-Malo to leave town. By the end of Part 9 the narrative has finally caught up to the beginning of the novel, as Werner catches and reads the same leaflet that Marie-Laure found in Part 0.

All the Light We Cannot See Analysis Chapters 148-165 (Part 10: 12 August 1944) Summary and Analysis

Summary

Part 10: 12 August 1944

148: Entombed

Werner listens to the girl read the story, in which the characters are trapped inside the submarine and they are worried they will asphyxiate. Then they travel north along the coast of South America, where they are attacked by a giant squid. Werner goes over to Volkheimer with the radio and places the headphones on his head. He says to him that he wishes he understood French, because it's a strange and beautiful story. Werner admits that the girl reading is using the transmitter they should have found, and that Werner knew about it all along, and wants to know if Volkheimer knew. Volkheimer is silent, and Werner thinks he possibly cannot hear him through the headphones. Werner feels he saved her just to hear her die, as she begs for help. Werner takes the headphones back and continues listening to the narrative about the crews fight against the monsters.

149: Fort National

Etienne begs the jailers to let him go so he can look after his blind niece. He tells them his papers were seized and he is 63, not 60, but no one can do anything. They can see the city burning across the water. After the stray American shell strikes Fort National and kills 9 men there, Etienne is quiet; he convinces himself he can see his house still standing through the smoke. He has neither pillow nor blanket, and they aren't given enough food. He fantasizing about escaping. They see and hear shells crashing into the sea. He thinks about how, during the last war, he knew men who could tell what a shell had hit by looking at the colors in the sky. He remembers listening to his first radio in Monsieur Hebrard's workshop; his brother Henri's voice, his parents, his house, all of it is burning now, he thinks. He looks at the fire and thinks that the universe is full of fuel.

150: Captain Nemo's Last Words

Marie-Laure has read 7 of the last 9 chapters of *TwentyThousand Leagues Under the Sea.* After escaping the giant squid, the submarine goes into a hurricane, and later, Captain Nemo steers it into a warship full of men. She hopes she brought some comfort to someone by reading the story, like her great uncle or some Americans. She has heard the German shout in frustration twice downstairs. She considers going through the wardrobe and handing the diamond to him, wondering if that will save her. She wonders what would happen if the goddess removed the curse—if this would all go away, perhaps. In the book, the characters see a moment to escape, and they agree if they are caught they are going to defend themselves, together. She turns on the transmitter and continues reading, thinking of the whelks in the grotto, hiding, protected from the gulls that would pick them up and break them open on the rocks.

151: Visitor

Von Rumpel worries he has made a mistake. Perhaps the Sea of Flames was in the museum all along, or the girl took it with her when Claude Levitte marched her away, or the old man had it in his rectum. Or perhaps it was never a real stone at all. He was certain he had gotten rid of all the obstacles. He hears the voice of his father telling him he is only being tested. Outside, a German corporal calls out to see if anyone is there, and informs von Rumpel that the city is being evacuated, that the Germans still hold the Chateau and Bastion de la Hollande, but that all other personnel are falling back. There will be a ceasefire at noon tomorrow to get the civilians out, and then bombing will resume. He asks which unit von Rumpel is with; von Rumpel directs the corporal to continue his work, telling him that he is almost done.

152: Final Sentence

Werner has not heard the broadcast in over an hour, and assumes the last sentence he heard was the last line of the book, which stated that only the narrator and Captain Nemo know the answer to a question asked by Ecclesiastes: "That which is far off, and exceeding deep, who can find it out?" He has felt deep hunger over the past days, but it seems to have left him now. Above him, Werner sees the Viennese girl in her cape, carrying a bag of withered greens. She floats down and settles herself in the rubble. She begins to list off offenses she committed, such as arguing over bread or not organizing her things according to protocol. He realizes she is Frau Schwartzenberger, the Jewish woman from Frederick's building. The last item she lists is "for failure of imagination"—and Werner feels he is at the bottom, like the Nautilus sucked under the maelstrom, or like his father in Zollverein. The ghost comes toward him and turns into the girl again, with the black hole in her forehead, into which he looks and sees a dark city full of souls. Her hears thunder and lightening; his organs shake; the beams shake; he hears the slow breath of Volkheimer.

153: Music #1

Sometime after midnight on August 13th, Marie-Laure decides she will put the record on. She has survived now without water for a day and a half, and without food for two. She still has the one can, but she hasn't opened it yet. She places it beneath the piano bench, where she will remember its location. She turns on the microphone and transmitter. She will turn the music up as loud as it can go, and if the German is still there he will find her. She begins to play the record. In her mind she walks a path in Jardin des Plantes, her father's hand stretched out to her. She crawls to the top of the ladder and sits with the house in one pocket and the knife in her hand, thinking, "Come and get me."

154: Music #2

In the city, everything sleeps, except for the snails and the rats. Werner sleeps in the ruins, but Volkheimer is awake. He has the radio on his lap with the headphones, but only because it is where Werner left them and he doesn't have the will to push them off. He is convinced the heads in the corner will kill him if he moves. Suddenly Werner hears music. As he listens to the music, he has a memory of walking in the woods with his grandfather. He puts the headphones on Werner's ears, who identifies the song, "Clair de Lune." Volkheimer tells Werner to hook the light to the battery, and he does, before the song is even over. Volkheimer drags sections of wall out of the rubble, stacking them into a barrier, and then pulls the cord to light the fuse of the grenade, throwing it at the place where the stairwell was.

155: Music #3

Von Rumpel remembers his daughters as children: as fat babies who then grew to little girls, who would sing songs for him with lyrics whose meaning was too mature for them to understand. He sees Veronika marching a doll in a white gown, with another in a gray suit, down the streets of the model city; they are met by a third doll in black at the cathedral—he's unsure if it is a wedding or a sacrifice. He hears Veronika singing softly, but it sounds more like piano. Somewhere above him a young Frenchman starts speaking about coal.

156: Out

For a moment, Werner cannot breath; the barrier collapses. But when he stops coughing, he sees Volkheimer staring up into a sliver of sky. Volkheimer goes up and clears the way, his hands bleeding, and they emerge into the rubble. Only two walls stand. Outside, there is only rubble and silence. Werner thinks of the nine men, or more, buried there in the hotel ruins. Volkheimer tells Werner to take the rifle and go. Volkheimer is going to find food. Werner moves through the city, thinking of the French girl whispering, "he will kill me." He sees a building with broken glass and hanging signs. He thinks of Bastian telling him he would strip the hesitation out of him, asking who is the weakest.

157: Wardrobe

Von Rumpel wobbles in front of the wardrobe, holding a candle, seeing the decades-old boys' clothes inside. He sees the trails in the dust and hears the voice from the ceiling; he leans in to observe closer just as two bells ring, one above him and one below him. He knocks his head on the wardrobe; the candle falls, and he lands on his back. He wonders if this is how death will come. The candle rolls towards the curtains. Someone steps inside the house.

158: Comrades

Werner enters the house and treads over broken crockery. He climbs all the stairs and sees each floor littered with ash and broken parts of doll houses, paper, bottles, and cords. On the sixth floor the stairs end and there are three doors. He enters the one to the right, which is a bedroom. He wonders if he is too late. He props the rifle against the bed and drinks from the water. Behind him he hears a voice say "ah," and he turns around to find a German officer, who looks pale and sick. He recognizes him from in front of the bakery. The way the officer smiles at him; Werner realizes he thinks they came for the same thing. Werner sees the fire of the curtain across the way, and mentions it to the officer. The officer talks instead about the ceasefire scheduled for noon tomorrow. He says he is the only one who knows where the thing is that they want, pointing his pistol at the ceiling and asking, "Is it up there?" Werner hopes the curtain fire will go out on its own. He thinks of the men with transmitters whom they killed, the looks on their faces like they had caught the tune of a familiar song. The German officer points the pistol at Werner's chest. Suddenly, they both hear a clattering, something bouncing down a ladder, and the sergeant major's attention goes toward the noise; Werner thinks to himself, "all your life you wait, and then it finally comes, and are you ready?"

159: The Simultaneity of Instants

Marie-Laure makes her way down the ladder, half-falling; pressing her ear against the wardrobe, she hears footsteps, hesitant, lighter than the sergeant major's. He opens the wardrobe door and she grips the knife tighter. The narration zooms out to Volkheimer, who sits by the sea in ruins, eating tinned yams. Then the narration switches to the wife of von Rumpel, who observes the good looks of an injured neighbor back from war. Then we see Jutta at Children's Home, then the führer eating breakfast, and then two inmates in Kiev. Then we see wagtail bird looking for snails to eat. Then we see young boys st Schulpforta waiting to receive antitank landmines, who will use them to defend a bridge in Russia and be killed by the tanks. Back at the wardrobe, Werner hears Marie-Laure inhale inside, and asks, in French, "*es tu la*?"—"are you there?"

160: Are You There?

Werner says to Marie-Laure that he hears her on the radio and he isn't there to kill her. The narrator says that all of us came here as a single cell, multiplied, and became beings. Marie-Laure comes out of the wardrobe; she tells Werner she cannot find her shoes.

161: Second Can

Marie-Laure sits in a corner with her heels tucked underneath her. Werner watches her movements, trying to make sure he remembers her forever. He says there is a ceasefire at noon, and she asks if he is sure; he is not. She asks what day it is; he does not know. He brings her water from the other room, where he tries not to look at von Rumpel's body. He tells her he used to hear the broadcasts on the radio. She tells him it was the voice of her grandfather. She goes up the ladder and brings down the can; she asks if Werner can tell what it is, but it has no label. He opens it, and the sweet perfume of peaches fills the air. She tells him she will share, as thanks for what he did. They devour the peaches; Werner feels like it's a sunrise in his mouth.

162: Birds of America

Werner is fascinated by all the books and wonders in the house, and he's fascinated by Marie-Laure. Marie-Laure shows him the transmitter and the old record that has her grandfather's voice. He asks her if she thinks that Captain Nemo survived the maelstrom; she says she doesn't know but she hopes so, because even though he was crazy she didn't want him to die. Werner finds the Audubon book of birds, the same one Frederick had, and asks if he can keep one of the pages. They know they need to go to lower ground, so eventually make their way down to the cellar. The floor booms from 30 bombs dropped miles away. Werner imagines how to prolong this moment, what their life would be like in 3 or 10 years when they could live in France or Germany and leave the house and eat at a tourist restaurant. Down in the cellar, Marie-Laure asks him if he knows why the man upstairs was there; he says he doesn't know, but suggests he might have come for the radio. And she says that perhaps that's why. They both fall asleep.

163: Cease-fire

Werner wakes first; the shelling has stopped. He watches Marie-Laure for a moment, then wakes her too. He finds her a pair of shoes in the house, and they stand at the doorstep, not sure of what is on the other side. He thinks of the entrance exam where he had to jump from the platform. They go outside, the streets smoking. He begins to see other civilians leaving their homes with suitcases and children. At one intersection Marie-Laure asks the street name, then takes him down a series of streets to the grotto, which she unlocks and enters with him. He tells her they need to leave, as the other civilians are leaving. He watches her touch the walls as if she were greeting old friends. She takes a small wooden object out of her pocket and places it in the water. She asks him to confirm it is the ocean, and that the object is in the water. He leads her out to the streets, and points her in the direction where he believes the collection point is. He tells her to walk that way holding out the white pillowcase he took from the house. She asks if he can come, but he knows it will not be good for her to be associated with him. She can't see him, but he feels he can't bear her gaze. They say goodbye, and she places something in his hand. He watches her walk away before opening his hand—an iron key is inside.

164: Chocolate

Madame Ruelle finds Marie-Laure in the old school where they are keeping refugees. The Americans have boxes of confiscated German chocolate, and they both eat more than they can count. A day later, the Americans gather the Frenchmen at Fort National. Madame Ruelle pulls Etienne out of the processing line, and he hugs Marie-Laure. The next day the Americans, gas the last German hold on Saint-Malo, and the Germans raise the white flag. When people are permitted back in the city, Madame Ruelle goes in to check in her bakery, but Marie-Laure and Etienne travel on to Rennes, where they rent a hotel room and separately take 2-hour hot baths. That night Etienne says to Marie-Laure that she can show him Paris.

165: Light

Werner is caught a few miles south of Saint Malo by French resistance fighters who initially think he's an old man because of his white hair. They later turn him over to Americans who have set up in a hotel. He is worried they will take him down to a cellar, but they take him upstairs instead. He is interviewed through an interpreter; he tries to ask about Marie-Laure, but his comment is brushed off. He thinks of Marie-Laure, of all of the details of her, and worries he will wear the images out. He is brought into a holding area with other Germans, but Volkheimer isn't there. Werner eats the soup that night, but later is sick. In the morning he also cannot keep the soup down. They are marched east to join a larger group in a warehouse. Medics try giving Werner gruel, but it won't stay in his stomach—the last thing that stayed down were the peaches. He wears Marie-Laure's uncles tweeds, and thinks of her with longing. He has a fever; he knows if he does not eat he will die, but when he eats he feels he will die. Later they are marched to Dinan. Many of the prisoners are young boys or older men, unknown to each other, all of them having seen things they wish to forget. On September 1st, Werner cannot get out of bed, and is taken to the medical tent. He stays there for a week, clutching his duffel in one hand and the little wooden house in the other. He figured out how to solve the puzzle of the house, and thinks it is very cleverly built. Other men in the tent are dying. In English the nurse and medic talk of his fever and how he won't eat. In dreams he sees the miners' lanterns; he sees Jutta inside a submarine. One night he sits up in bed and sees clouds in the sky outside of the tent flaps. He sees Frau Elena by a stove, with an infant Jutta nearby; he feels the webbing of Marie-Laure's fingers against his own. He hears Volkheimer's voice saying "What you could be." He gets up out of bed. Werner remembers a time when he and Jutta built a boat; when they put it on the water it was swallowed by the current, and he told her they would build another.

Now he tries to remember whether they actually did. He walks outside into the moonlight. Across the field an American watches a boy leave the tent, and he tries to stop him; however, when Werner reaches the edge of the field he steps on a landmine planted by his own army months before, and disappears in a fountain of earth.

Analysis

Part 10 contains the climax of the novel: Werner is trapped and is looking for a way to get out, and Marie-Laure is trapped in the attic hiding with the Sea of Flames; at the same time, Werner listens to Marie-Laure read *Twenty Thousand Leagues Under the Sea* on the radio. In Marie-Laure's protective shell of the attic, the motif of the whelk as Marie-Laure is demonstrated. In fact, she uses her imagination to conjure imagery of her snails in the grotto who are also protecting themselves by hiding there so that gulls do not cause them harm.

The motif of vision and sight was brought in with Werner's ability to see in the dark in Part 8, and now Volkheimer too is beginning to see through the darkness, albeit in a delirious way, believing the white heads he can see will kill him. Thus, he too is haunted in his own way by what he has been a part of. Unlike Werner, who is motivated by his guilt and his desire to save Marie-Laure, Volkheimer is paralyzed by his. He is sitting, unmoving, with the radio on his ears. He has given up hope—until he hears the music from the radio.

Marie-Laure's belief in the Sea of Flames curse is apparent when she wonders what would happen if the goddess removed the curse. Like her father, she was initially skeptical, but the chaos around her seems so much like a curse. However, Chapter 141 also reveals that Etienne did survive the shelling of Fort National, and thus there is still hope that perhaps Marie-Laure is not cursed.

The narrative of Captain Nemo and Professor Aronnax is being told in parallel to the rising climax of the novel, as both Werner and Marie-Laure struggle to survive; the characters in *Twenty Thousand Leagues Under the Sea*, Marie-Laure, and Werner are all trapped and facing obstacles to their survival. Yet, both Werner and Marie-Laure make it out of their respective traps alive; in contrast, *Twenty Thousand Leagues Under the Sea* ends in a question, where neither the reader, nor Marie-Laure, nor Werner knows what the fate of Captain Nemo and Professor Aronnax were as they went into a maelstrom.

Chapter 152 is called the Final Sentence, which has multiple meanings. The first is the literal meaning: the final sentence of the book that Marie-Laure finished reading, which has left Werner wondering what happens to the characters. *Twenty Thousand Leagues Under the Sea* ends on a question from the Bible. This part of the Bible discusses the limits of human wisdom. In addition to the Final Sentence of the book,

Werner also sees the apparitions of the Viennese Girl and Frau Schwartzenberger. The Viennese girl, who received her final sentence of death at the hands of Werner's unit, and he has been carrying her with him in a ghost form ever since. In regard to Frau Schwartzenberger, her fate is unknown, but as this apparition she lists off a series of offenses that would have been offenses she was accused of in a concentration camp; thus her appearing is a symbol for all the Jewish people killed at the hands of the Nazis, and Werner is charged with this guilt as well. As he looks into the hole in the head of the little girl, inside he sees the souls of millions of people, the victims of the genocide he participated in by being a part of the Nazi army. The final sentence of the offenses Frau Schwartzenberger apparition lists is "for failure of imagination"; in contrast to the power of imagination, which has allowed Werner to escape the terrible reality around him, and which has also allowed him success in his pursuit of science and technology, Frau Schwartzenberger has not been able to use imagination as an escape. Werner at this moment feels as if he too is in the bottom of the sea: he parallels the experiences of Captain Nemo and of his father, dying in the coal mine, metaphorically completely crushed by the darkness he has participated in.

The climax of the novel occurs when Werner escapes from the cellar and goes to save Marie-Laure from von Rumpel. Finally, he has a chance to make the humanist choice of choosing his own destiny, acting outside of his duties but in the nature of kindness and compassion for another human being. Humanism is defined by Merriam Webster as "a doctrine, attitude, or way of life centered on human interests or values; especially: a philosophy that usually rejects supernaturalism and stresses an individual's dignity and worth and capacity for self-realization through reason." Doerr has said that his novel is a humanistic perspective on how people can be kind in spite of the circumstances. Werner's saving Marie-Laure is the ultimate act of humanism portrayed in the novel: that of a character whose ideals are supposedly completely opposite of another's, but who acts out of love and kindness toward the other regardless.

Marie-Laure and Werner thus have the moment of meeting that the entire novel has been leading up to, Werner is in love with Marie-Laure, and Marie-Laure sees in Werner more than just a Nazi soldier: she sees a boy who came to save her life, a kind soul, someone with whom she wants to share Madame Manec's peaches. Despite Marie-Laure's blindness, Werner too detects that she can see into him, which is why he can't bear her gaze as he leaves her to go to safety while he has to stay behind.

Part 10 mysteriously ends with Werner stepping on a land mine; the reader at this point knows that Werner went into the grotto and collected the wooden house, and that he knows that it opens as a puzzle, which he thinks is clever. However, the suspense is built around where the Sea of Flames is: does Werner have it, and if so, how is it that he steps on a landmine? Is the protection of the stone real or fake? And if he does not have the stone, where is it?

All the Light We Cannot See Chapters 166-178 (Part 11: 1945, Part 12: 1974 & Part 13: 2014) Summary and Analysis

Summary

Part 11: 1945

166: Berlin

In January 1945, Frau Elena and the remaining 4 girls in the house—the twins, Hannah and Susanne Gerlitz, Claudia Forster, and Jutta, who is 15—are brought to Berlin to work in a machine parts factory for 10 hours a day, 6 days a week. Frau Elena wears an old ski parka. They live in an apartment above an old printing factory, burning pages from misprinted dictionaries. They are served food in the canteen, with limited portions of butter. Mothers have no diapers for their babies. Most of the girls cannot read, so Jutta reads them the letters they get from their relatives at the front, and sometimes writes responses for them. All spring the bombers come, and most nights they go to a cramped shelter. They see bodies in the street, sometimes burnt, sometimes looking like they are just asleep. Claudia stops talking. The mail stops. In March, there are no materials left. Jutta hears of boys who deserted and were then shot in the streets. She recalls memories with Werner, in their wagon. She receives two letters in the fall in Zollverein announcing his death, listing two different places of burial in France. She dreams of him having gears and belts on a table, announcing that he is making something. By April, women are talking of how the Russians are coming to seek revenge on them. The only good thing that happens in this period is that Claudia finds a box of 15 pastries, which they all eat giddily. Jutta hears that women are making their daughters as unattractive as possible, or drowning them, to avoid a worse fate at the hands of the Russians. The Russians come to their apartment one day in May. Frau Elena prays, and tells the girls she will go first. Four Russians come in: two officers and two young boys. All of them take their turns with each girl. Jutta's assailant says a list of Russian words out loud while he rapes her; she later decides he was saying the names of dead comrades. Before they leave, they shoot at the ceiling; plaster rains down. Frau Elena zips herself back into her parka, rubbing her arm in one spot as if trying to stay warm.

167: Paris

Etienne rents the same apartment in Paris where Marie-Laure and her father lived. He listens to the news about released prisoners; he petitions the repatriation authorities. They wait every day at the Gare d'Austerlitz train station. Sometimes Dr. Geffard comes to wait with them. He tells Marie-Laure that her return makes him believe that there is good in the world. She talks to officials at the museum, who assure her they are trying to find her father; they do not mention the Sea of Flames. In the spring, Berlin and Goring surrender. Parades happen spontaneously. Etienne tells Marie-Laure that they may never know what happened to her father. They wait at the train station all summer. One day in August, Marie-Laure leads them into the Jardin des Plantes. She cannot lift the hood of grief; yet she tells Etienne she would like to go to school.

Part 12: 1974

168: Volkheimer

Volkheimer, 52 years old, lives in an apartment in Pforzheim, West Germany, across from a billboard that reflects light into his apartment at night. He works as a TV antenna repairman. His apartment is barren, with only a few pieces of furniture and a TV. He has no family, no pets, and no plants. In his work he is quiet and solitary. He only feels at home on the windiest days. Sometimes in summer, his loneliness feels like a disease. He sees the eyes of men he killed. Before going to bed he checks his mail, which he has not checked in a week. There is a package with 3 photographs: 1 of a duffel, 1 of a small wooden house partially crushed, and 1 of a notebook. The letter explains that the organization is trying to deliver these items to the next of kin of an unknown soldier, and they believe Volkheimer knows who the soldier is. He thinks of how they were all only boys. He thinks of the boy with white hair and ears that stuck out. He thinks of how that boy asked him if it was decent to leave the dead prisoner outside like that. He knows who the items belong to.

169: Jutta

Jutta Wette, now married to Albert Wette, is an Algebra teacher in Essen. Her husband Albert is a kind, balding accountant, who loves running model trains in their basement. Jutta got pregnant at age 37, after years of believing she couldn't have children. They have a son named Max who is 6 years old. He loves to ask questions no one can answer, and make paper airplanes. He has ears that stick out. On a Thursday in June, they go to the pool, and then drive home. At home Albert prepares dinner while Jutta corrects exams, and Max makes paper airplanes. A knock at the door makes Jutta's heart pound. Max answers, and Jutta goes to meet a giant man at the door wearing a grey sweatsuit. He confirms that her maiden name is Pfennig. She knows that his business is about Werner. The giant ducks his head and comes inside their house, and Albert asks him to dinner. He slowly reveals the reason he came: he was contacted and he asked the organization if he could deliver the bag himself; he came several hours by train to bring it here. He tells them that he spent the last month of the war in Saint-Malo with Werner, and that he thinks Werner fell in love.

Jutta has spent years trying not to think of the war, especially not of those last months in Berlin. She sometimes looks at older female colleagues and wonders what they did when the electricity was out. She wants Volkheimer to leave and take the bag with him. She rarely allows herself to think of Werner. Albert asks Max to take Volkheimer outside to the patio for cake. Inside Albert asks if Jutta is all right, and he tells her he loves her. She looks out the window and sees Volkheimer patiently teaching Max to fold an advanced version of a paper airplane, which flies straight and true. Jutta tells Albert that she loves him too.

170: Duffel

After Volkheiemer leaves, Jutta puts Max to bed, and Albert goes to run his trains in the basement. She can hear the noise of them even upstairs. She takes the duffel upstairs and sets it by her desk while she tries to grade exams. She loses focus. She remembers how, when she first married Albert and he would go on business trips, she'd remember the pain she felt after Werner left for Schulpforta. She opens the duffel bag and finds a package wrapped in newspaper: a small wooden model house no bigger than her fist. She also finds the envelope with his childhood notebook that she sent him. She opens it and looks at the models of inventions he drew and the questions he wrote, such as "why do some fish have whiskers?". She closes the notebook as her memories come back to her. Then she reopens it and reads more. Between the last two pages she finds an envelope that says "For Frederick"—she knows this is for his bunkmate, the boy who loved birds. When her husbands comes to bed she pretends she is still grading exams.

171: Saint-Malo

Jutta decides to take her son to Saint-Malo during the summer break, convincing herself the trip is for him to see the sea and learn some French; she wants to go without her husband. Albert drives them to the train, and they depart. At one point a Frenchman with a prosthetic leg gets on the train and sits next to Jutta; she is worried he will accuse her of being the reason why he has a prosthetic leg, but he does not. They arrive in the night and check into a hotel in Saint-Malo. She is scared to try her French, so she skips dinner. In the morning Max pulls her around exploring the beach, looking up at the ramparts. Jutta cannot stop looking at the sea, thinking of the letter her brother wrote her, stating that the sea seemed to be be able to contain anything anyone ever felt. They climb the chateau and observe the old town, where she sees no traces of the bombings. They climb a quay in the Porte de Dinan, across from the old city. There are big steel caps where soldiers would have directed fire at the hill. There is a plaque in remembrance of a dead French boy, aged 18. Jutta thinks to herself that there are no plaques for the Germans who died here.

Jutta asks herself why she has come. On the second day, she takes the wooden house to the historical museum, and the man there brings her to see Number 4 rue Vauborel. The house now is divided into flats. She asks if there was a girl who lived there; he confirms that a blind girl lived there during the war, and that his mother told stories about her. She asks him why her brother would have had that model house, and the man suggests perhaps the girl would know. He offers to find her address. Max tries to get Jutta's attention: he thinks he has found a way to open the house.

172: Laboratory

Marie-Laure LeBlanc works in the Museum of Natural History in the study of mollusks. She has published successful papers. As a graduate student she went to Bora Bora and Bimini and collected snails in reefs. She is not a collector like Dr. Geffard; she prefers to be among living creatures. She and Etienne traveled while he still could—to Sardinia, Scotland, and to London. He died at age 82 and left her plenty of money. They looked into what happened to her father, but the only information they found was that, at a camp in Kessel, Germany, he contracted the flu in 1943. Marie-Laure still lives in the flat where she grew up. She has had two lovers. One was a visiting scientist who never came back. The other was a Canadian named John, who scattered items about any room he entered. They separated undramatically when she got pregnant, and they have a 19-year-old daughter named Helene, who is petit, and an aspiring violinist. All three still eat lunch together every Friday. Marie-Laure still has things she cannot tolerate that remind her of the war: shoes that are too big, boiled turnips, and lists of names that remind her of lists of prisoner names on which her father's name never appeared. She still counts storm drains to move around towns. She occasionally walks to a brasserie where she orders duck in honor of Dr. Geffard. She is happy for parts of every day: when she receives a package of shells; when she thinks of reading Jules Verne to her daughter. She also sometimes gets overwhelmed with the feeling that the museum is like a mausoleum, with all of its dead items classified in different rooms. This feeling happens rarely: she is reassured by her own gurgling salt water tanks. One Wednesday in July, her assistant says there is a woman with a child there to visit her. She asks what she looks like; the assistant says she has white hair and is badly dressed, and says she got her address from a museum in Brittany. Marie-Laure feels vertigo. She hears the tinkling of 10,000 keys on hooks behind her. She feels the room has tilted and she will slide off the edge.

173: Visitor

Marie-Laure says to Jutta, "You learned French as a child." Max introduces himself in German. Jutta tells her she brought something, and Marie-Laure knows it is the house. Marie-Laure asks her assistant Francis to take Max to see something in the museum for a moment. They leave, and, alone with Jutta, Marie-Laure touches the house. Jutta asks how her brother got it, wondering whether he stole it. Marie-Laure wonders if the house has ever been opened. She tells Jutta that her brother did not steal it: she and Werner spent a day together when she was 16. Jutta tells her he died. "Of course," Marie-Laure thinks: because he didn't fit into the after-war stories, of French resistance heroes, or of blond Germans watching broken cities from tank hatches, or terrible psychopathic Germans who tortured Jewesses. She remembers that he told her that he and his sister used to pick berries by the Ruhr. Marie-Laure says his hands were smaller than hers; Jutta says he was always small for his age, and that it was hard for him not to do what was expected of him. Marie-Laure wonders if he went back into the grotto to get the house, and whether he might have left the stone there. Marie-Laure tells Jutta that he told her that he and Jutta used to listen to her great-uncle's broadcasts together. At that moment Max and Francis come back. They decide to leave; Marie-Laure tells Jutta she will send her the last remaining copy of her grandfather's work, about the moon; she thinks that Max might like it.

174: Paper Airplane

Max tells Jutta what he learned at the museum. Jutta, tired, leans against a tree. They make their way back to their hotel. Max asks her if she showed the lady how the house opened; she says she thinks she already knew. She looks out over the houses in Paris, and thinks of the drawings she made as a child. A sports game is on TV. Max folds a paper airplane and launches it over the street. Jutta calls her husband.

175: The Key

Marie-Laure sits in her lab touching shells. She is filled with memories. She shakes the house, knowing it won't give away if something is inside. She wonders what kind of boy Werner was; she remembers him paging through the book of birds. She imagines him going back into the old kennel, finding the house, solving it, and letting the diamond drop into the sea, or keeping it, or putting it back in the house. She thinks of how Dr. Geffard once told her that the diamond is so valuable and so beautiful, it is hard to turn away from. She twists the chimney, and slides off the roof tiles, the first one of them sticking. A key slides out into her hand.

176: Sea of Flames

The narrator describes the process of the formation of the diamond: "from the molten basements of the world," old, hard, made by magma, rocks, ice, lakes, trees rising and falling. A storm one day brings the stone out of a canyon, and it catches the attention of a prince; it is cut and polished and passed through the hands of men. Now, it is described as a lump of carbon no larger than a chestnut, covered with algae, crawled on by snails.

177: Frederick

Frederick and his mother live in the middle floor of a triplex apartment building. Frederick mostly sits on the patio and watches the wind blow plastic bags, or draws thick, heavy-handed spirals. The house is full of them; his mother has given up on throwing them away. She has few people who come over. She has felt she needed to hide since the war; like many widows, she was made to feel that she was an accomplice in an unspeakable crime. In the mail on Wednesday, a letter comes for Frederick. Inside the envelope there is a letter from a woman explaining the course of the smaller envelope from France, to a prisoner of war camp, to a storage facility in New Jersey, to an organization in West Berlin. She shows Frederick the envelope with his name written in cursive. It is night; she turns on all of the lights to feel less lonely, and she makes dinner. She blends vegetables and rice and feeds them to Frederick, who hums while he eats, happy. Afterwards, she opens the envelope, which contains two birds in full color: the Aquatic Wood Wagtail. She remembers the day she bought that book for her son, how she knew he would love it. The doctors tell her he retains no memories, just basic functions, but she wonders. She shows him the pages; he looks at them and then returns to drawing. After she does the dishes, she takes him outside on the patio, their nightly ritual. Starlings are flying outside, and she sometimes thinks he perks up when he sees them. Tonight, a huge owl lands on the deck railing, and she thinks, "You've come for me." Frederick stares at it. Then it goes. She asks Frederick if he saw it. He says, "Mutti?" twice, and then asks her, "what are we doing?" She tells him that they are just sitting and looking out at the night.

Part 13: 2014

178

Marie-Laure lives to see the turn of the century. On a Saturday in March, her grandson Michel comes to get her from her apartment and takes her walking in the Jardin des Plantes. There is still ice on the ground, and when she reaches a puddle with a thin layer of ice, she stops and tries to lift it up whole. The boy is patient and waits for her. They climb to the northwest corner of the gardens, and sit on a bench. No one else is there, perhaps because of the cold. Marie-Laure states to him that he will be 12 next Saturday. He is excited because he will get to ride the moped. He plays a game on a device next to her, and then loses, telling her that he died but can start again. He asks her what she wanted for her 12th birthday, and she says that she wanted a book by Jules Verne. He asks if it is the same book his mother read him, with the complicated fish names and lots of mollusks. She thinks of the waves traveling into Michel's machine, the torrents of text conversations, commercials, and mail, crossing in the air. She wonders if it is possible, too, that souls might travel those same paths—Etienne, her father, Madame Manec, the German boy named Werner Pfennig, passing in and out of the air, with a record of every life lived still reverberating. Michel walks her back to her building; they say goodbye. She listens to his footsteps fade, to cars and trains, and to people hurrying in the cold.

Analysis

Part 11 is a short section set in 1945 to summarize the rest of World War II for two of the surviving characters, Marie-Laure and Jutta. Chapter 66, set in Berlin, is one of the first sections in which the omniscient narrator takes on Jutta's narration. The chapter explores the theme of darkness and light from a slightly different lens: up until now, passages about Jutta have fallen into the light/good side of this spectrum due to her opposition to the war and her apparent ethical purity. However, she, like Werner, is also surrounded by darkness: not because she is participating in the war as directly as Werner chose to, but rather because the darkness was inescapable for any German at that time. The chapter is an exposition of the type of life a German woman may have been subjected to at the time. The chapter is bleak, with a mood of despair and a tense suspenseful quality of waiting for something terrible to happen: the girls are starving, unsure of whether they will survive the constant bombing, and unsure of when the encroaching Russians will appear. In the end, the Russians do appear, and in a tone just as matter-of-fact and dark as the rest of the chapter, the narrator states bluntly: "The Russians come for them on a cloudless day in May," and raped all of them.

Marie-Laure and Etienne have depressed and odd mood as well, as Marie-Laure returns to Paris and finds it different. Marie-Laure still copes with the loss of her father, never finding out any information about his disappearance. However, she has the will to survive through the strength she finds in two of the major themes: familial loyalty, through Etienne and her former mentor Dr. Geffard, and science and technology—for at the end of the chapter, she decides, despite her grief, to return to school.

In Part 12, 1974, the narrative of Volkheimer echoes the last version Werner saw of him: like Atlas, holding the world on his shoulders in the cellar of the Hotel of Bees; he still carries guilt, and his loneliness is compared in a simile to a disease. Jutta, too, is wracked with guilt, despite the fact that she was ethically against the Nazi party. However, as demonstrated by the lightness and darkness theme, there is a lot of gray area in between goodness and evil, and how people make their choices is what determines their destiny. Jutta, Volkheimer, and Frederick's mother were all part of a greater whole of the German people whose collective choices lead to the damage done; thus, all of them feel guilt, regardless of their varying levels of participation.

Jutta's son Max is in many ways an image of Werner, although the comparison is not directly made by Jutta and is only implied in the narration; it is implied in the imagery and description of Max, who has ears that stick out, and who has a curiosity and cleverness like Werner had as a child. In fact, Max is the one who discovers that the little house opens.

Memory is the heaviest theme of Part 12: Volkheimer, Jutta and Marie-Laure are called back into the time of the war by the objects that were included in Werner's belongings. While memory during the war chapters was often used as a form of escape for the characters to more pleasant times, here it has changed. The times that these pieces—the miniature house, the notebook—call up are of a time that is not pleasant. They recall memories that the characters almost don't want to have, thus the imagery surrounding them is of the memories escaping, overflowing, or of being very hot.

The very last chapter is from the familiar narrative of Marie-Laure, but this time she is an old woman, with her grandson of a completely different generation. This leads her to reflect on the transferring of information, which through this book has been mostly through radio. In 2014, however, technology has advanced, and now her grandson uses an electronic device to play a handheld game. In an interview, Anthony Doerr said, "Radio... was how larger political and artistic narratives entered the homes of people, and it held power over children in much the way tablets and smartphones hold power over children now" (Smith). Thus Doerr uses this last, more modern chapter to tie in a current thread of how internet plays a role in influencing the minds of youth. In addition, Marie-Laure ties in the theme of memory and imagination, as well as her ironic ability to see, as she wonders whether the souls of lost people use those same radio or cellular waves to travel through time and remain with us.

All the Light We Cannot See Symbols, Allegory and Motifs

Sight and Vision (motif)

From the title page to the very last page of the novel, sight and vision are a strong motif. Marie-Laure LeBlanc has obvious vision problems stemming from her blindness, yet she can clearly see things invisible to others, like morality and intellect. Contrasting with LeBlanc is Werner Pfenning, whose perfect vision is a requirement for acceptance into the National Institute, yet who constantly finds himself in a struggle to see the ugly reality behind the whitewashed veneer of the Nazi Party.

The Curse (allegory) of The Sea of Flames (symbol)

What a fantastically resonant symbol the Sea of Flames diamond is: the true value lies not in the sparkling cuts, but rather in the belief that whoever owns it is endowed with eternal life. Further enhancing the complexity of this symbol is the allegory surrounding it, that the price to pay for that eternal life of the owner is the deaths of those whom the owner cherishes most. Ultimately, the diamond is invested with great symbolic currency because it proves to have only the value of crystallized carbon, despite the other values that people try to impose on it.

The curse of the diamond provides an interesting allegory throughout the course of the story. The original story of the curse is that a goddess of the earth intended the stone as a gift for the ocean, but a prince took it from a riverbed and it never reached its destination. Because the stone gives the holder eternal life, it saved his life when attacked, but slowly all those around him began to perish and his kingdom was attacked. A priest warned him of the danger of keeping the stone because of the curse of the goddess, but the prince had the priest's tongue cut out. The meaning behind the allegory is multiple: for instance, (1) those who speak the truth are punished (the priest); and (2) what is eternal life worth, without those who love you around to share it?

Whelks (symbol)

Marie-Laure gives herself the code name "The Whelk" when she joins the French Resistance. Her symbolic association with not just whelks, but mollusks in general, permeates throughout the novel. Marie-Laure is a respected scientist who specializes in the study of mollusks. The symbolic association between her and the mollusk is characterized most strongly by her admiration of their ability to withstand the damage inflicted on them by seagulls, and their ability to stay connected to surfaces against which the water ceaselessly bangs. It is the stability, tenacity, and constancy of the whelks that makes them a fitting symbol for the protagonist.

Models and Puzzles (symbol)

Daniel LeBlanc builds intricate models of cities for the blind Marie-Laure as means of creating a navigable 3-D map for her to determine where she lives and how to get around there. In this way, Marie-Laure can find her way through the city in a way that even those with sight and vision cannot: she doesn't need the street signs or other written cues indicating location, geography, and topography. On a small scale, these models become symbols for the ways in which the characters are forced to traverse unknown geographies, but as the novel moves on, the symbolic depth expands to comment on the various ways in which people try to reduce more complex concepts down to more manageable laws and rules.

Radio Transmission (motif)

Eventually it becomes clear that the radio show that Werner loves so much features the transmission of the narration by none other than Henri LeBlanc: Marie-Laure's grandfather. The twin narrative threads that make up the story ultimately are directly connected most strongly by the motifs of vision and transmission of information. The radio is the source of transmission that binds Werner and Marie-Laure together. The radio transmissions of Marie-Laure's grandfather become the catalyst driving him to save her life, so in a sense, the radio itself ultimately becomes the symbolic representation of the light that cannot be seen.

All the Light We Cannot See Metaphors and Similes

"The fires pool and strut; they flow up the sides of the ramparts like tides; they splash into alleys, over rooftops, through a carpark. Smoke chases dust; ash chases smoke. A newsstand floats, burning." (Ch 32) (metaphor and simile)

Metaphor and simile are used here to draw a parallel between the fire of the bombings of Saint-Malo and water. This describes how the flames seem to move and flow as if they were water. Also, this description alludes to the name of the precious diamond, the Sea of Flames, and how it contains in its name water and fire, their relationship inseparable. On top of this, the metaphors here are used to highlight the living nature of the flames and ash, personifying them.

"Marie-Laure looks up from her book and believes she can smell gasoline under the wind. As if a great river of machinery is steaming slowly, irrevocably, toward her." (Ch 23) (simile)

This is a simile for the war that is coming to take over France and is unstoppable. There is metonymy here in the use of the machinery, because it implies more than just the literal tanks and weapons: it is also the machinery of Nationalism, the ideology that has lead Germany to invade France. Marie-Laure is trapped in this reality; this is emphasized by her helplessness conveyed in this simile, because the movement is irrevocable.

"Radio: it ties a million ears to a single mouth. Out of loudspeakers all around

Zollverein, the staccato voice of the Reich grows like some imperturbable tree; its subjects lean toward its branches as if toward the lips of God." (Ch 24) (simile)

This simile highlights the power of radio in the spreading of nationalist propaganda of the Third Reich. The voice grows like a tree, evoking imagery of something that is strong and well-rooted. The subjects (the Germans) lean as if toward the lips of God; the simile thus builds on the initial image to liken the voice of the Third Reich to that of God, because the ideology is revered and worshipped.

"One hundred children passing sleek and interchangeable in their white uniforms like livestock before the eyes of the examiners." (ch 38) (simile)

The examiners in the entrance exams are observing the children as if they were animals being evaluated for purity of lineage and ableness of body, as if they were animals to be bred like livestock. This simile underlines the nationalist ideology of the purity and conformity, as symbolized by the white uniforms.

"Memory coming at Werner like a six-car train out of the darkness...The recognition is immediate. It is as if he has been drowning for as long as he can remember and somebody has fetched him up for air." (Ch 133) (simile)

When Werner listens to the radio and hears the voice of Etienne—much like that of "The Professor" to whom Werner used to listen, combined with the music Clair de Lune—he feels assaulted by the memory at first, hence the comparison to being hit by an unexpected train... Yet as he listens more, he begins to feel relief, as if in the time between when he once knew that voice and this moment, he has been suffering or drowning. This suffering was the ideology of the Third Reich, in the actions he has committed that further their cruel goals; hearing these familiar sounds is like breathing again, reminding him of the good he once knew in himself.

All the Light We Cannot See Irony

The location of the Sea of Flames (dramatic irony)

There is dramatic irony in the changing location of the diamond, the Sea of Flames: the reader is almost always kept abreast of where the diamond is, yet the characters often are not aware of this, or they are oblivious to the diamond's presence. For example, as von Rumpel searches for it, the reader is aware of its presence with Daniel LeBlanc. Also, in the beginning of the novel, Marie-Laure shows the reader the location of the diamond in 1944: inside the model house of Number 4 rue Vauborel. However, as the novel goes back in time, it reveals that Marie-Laure only discovers the location of the diamond shortly before the bombings of Saint-Malo. In the end, the reader is also shown where the diamond ultimately resides, though no living character knows this.

Marie-Laure's ability to "see" (situational irony)

"Marie-Laure knows this even though her back is to him, even though he says nothing, even though she is blind—Papa's thick hair is wet from the snow and standing in a dozen angles off his head, and his scarf is draped asymmetrically over his shoulders, and he's beaming up at the falling snow." (ch 15, light)

Although Marie is technically blind, she is one of the most perceptive characters in the book. Through her other senses and her memory, she constructs an emotional and visceral reality for the reader more so than any other character in the book.

Werner joined the military to have a different fate from his father, killed in a mine; yet he ends up trapped in a small confined space (dramatic irony)

Werner makes the decision to join the military, despite his doubts, because he does not want to end up in the same fate as his father, who died trapped inside a coal mine, his body never recovered. Although he realized that Schulpforta and the cruel nationalist ideology are wrong, he does not turn away from them, partially in fear of the fate that would await him if he were to go back to Zollverein. We see this when Werner struggles after finding out Frederick has been beaten so badly he won't be coming back to Schulpforta: "In the hall with the door shut behind him, Werner presses his forehead against the wall, and a vision of his father's last moments comes to him, the crushing press of the tunnels, the ceiling lowering. Jaw pinned against the floor. Skull splintering. I cannot go home, he thinks. And I cannot stay" (Ch 85). However, in the Saint-Malo bombing in 1944, despite his efforts to avoid the same fate as his father, Werner ends up trapped in the cellar of a hotel, with no way out.

Werner's letter to Jutta in which he states his mistakes, but all of the the mistakes are censored—the only phrase remaining is his saying that he hopes she understands (dramatic irony)

"Frederick used to say there is no such thing as free will and that every person's path is predetermined for him just like X and that my mistake was that I X X X X X X X X X X X X . I hope someday you can understand." (Ch 88).

Werner has begun to realize that the decision he made to go into the military was a decision: he was responsible for his actions, and Jutta was right in her opposition to his joining the military. He reflects on what Frederick said to him, and earnestly writes this in a letter to her—yet, the substance of the letter was deemed unfit by the censor, and thus was blacked out. In this moment when Werner is attempting to make things right with his sister, instead she just receives a bunch of blacked out sentences, which ironically ends with "I hope someday you can understand": there is not enough information there for her to understand much of anything.

All the Light We Cannot See Imagery

"In his hand, the stone is about the size of a chestnut. Even at this late hour, in the quarter-light, it glows a majestic blue. Strangely cold" (Ch 31)

The Sea of Flames plays an important role in the novel, for its value as a gem as well as its value as an object that holds the power of eternal life. The imagery surrounding the Sea of Flames endows it with a magical element: it usually glows, changes color, and has unexpected weight or temperature, thus emphasizing its mysterious power.

"And as night falls, Werner pulls little Jutta wordlessly back through the close-set neighborhoods of Zollverein, two snowy-haired children in a bottomland of soot" (Ch 10)

Werner and Jutta's white hair is juxtaposed with the dark imagery of the depressing coal-mining town where they live. Werner and Jutta, in their adventures and devotion to each other, seem to embody the color of their hair: their whiteness makes them good and pure. Later, Jutta embodies this in her moral and ethical opposition to what Germany is doing; on the opposite side, Werner embodies this in his purity of hair and skin, which is the image of what Nazi Germany would like to look like.

"Color—that's another thing people don't expect. In her imagination, in her dreams, everything has color" (Ch 17); "That little attic bursting with bursting with magenta and aquamarine and gold for five minutes,

and then the radio switches off, and the gray rushes back in, and her uncle stumps back down the stairs" (Ch 113)

Although Marie-Laure is blind, she feels color in the objects, places, and people around her. Thus, her world is not at all dark, but rather full of the colors she dreams and imagines. However, near the end of the war, as the mood in Saint-Malo darkens Marie-Laure feels only gray, the only thing lighting up Marie-Laure's world is hearing her great-uncle's resistance broadcasts with their music.

"It sucks and booms and splashes and rumbles; it shifts and dilates and falls over itself; the labyrinth of Saint-Malo has opened onto a portal of sound larger than anything she has ever experienced" (Ch 71); "It contains so many colors. Silver at dawn, green at noon, dark blue in the evening. Sometimes it looks almost red. Or it will turn the color of old coin" (Ch 132, Letter from Werner to Jutta)

The ocean is Marie-Laure and Werner's favorite thing; both of them find comfort and pleasure in the sensory delights it provides. In Marie-Laure's first trip to the ocean, she is impressed by the vastness of its sound and size, and by the creatures and objects she finds in the sand. It helps to heal her from the heartache of losing her father. For Werner, the ocean reminds him how to feel: he is impressed by the amount of colors it contains, how they change, and how it seems to him that it could contain anything anyone could ever feel.

All the Light We Cannot See Humanism in All the Light We Cannot See

Anthony Doerr's World War II narrative *All the Light We Cannot See* was on the New York Times' Bestseller list for over 100 weeks straight. It has become an important part of the canon of World War II literature. The book focuses on the way war impacts the lives of children, and on finding the goodness where it seems there is none.

In an interview with Scribner, Doerr asks, "Could I tell a story about how a promising boy got sucked into the Hitler Youth and made bad decisions that led to terrible, unforgivable consequences, yet still render him an empathetic character?" Anthony Doerr wanted to write a story that conveyed *humanism*. Humanism is a progressive philosophy of life that, without theism and other supernatural beliefs, affirms our ability and responsibility to lead ethical lives of personal fulfillment that aspire to the greater good of humanity ("Definition of Humanism").

However, strangely for a book set in World War II, there is no extensive mention of the Holocaust. Only one Jewish character is named, and her story is only briefly mentioned. This has aroused some rancor amongst readers; in a scathing review of Doerr's novel in *The New Republic*, Green denounces Doerr for normalizing the Holocaust, stating Doerr's novel is an unsavory mixture of "relativizing" and "aestheticizing." Green claims that Doerr presents all violence, Nazi or Allied, as equivalent. Similarly, in the online publication *On Reform Judaism*, Halpern questions whether this is a new trend in World War II literature: the narrative of the sympathetic Nazi, as seen in *The Book Thief* as well. Yet, both these critics' opinions, as well as Doerr's recognition that Werner's narrative is emotionally harrowing and complicated, fit well with the idea that in modern historical fiction there is "recognition that all experience is subjective and every narrative partial" (Maragonis).

Doerr admits Werner's was not an easy perspective to write from, saying "Part of the reason the book took me so long to write was that the subject matter was distressing" (Panda). Yet, Werner's narrative is balanced by Marie-Laure's all-seeing goodness. Werner is presented as a person victimized by his environment: he is a victim his poverty, lack of family, his natural adolescent desire to belong, and the nationalist propaganda inundating Germany at the time. Werner's story thus asks the reader to consider how this type of historical retelling can help us grapple with the ethical complications of the past (Heyer & Fidyk). Specifically, what is our role as humans in making ethical choices, in the effort to shape our own destiny? Werner is an example of someone who is an inextricable part of horrible atrocities, and yet he remains very much relatable and sympathetic. Doerr, in his interviews, talks of humanism and how it influenced his novel, which is about "the ways in which people, against all odds, try to be kind to one another" ("All the Light We Cannot See FAQ"). In the end, Werner's character comes to believe in and embody humanism, despite his affiliation with the Nazi party: he realizes he has choices in his own destiny, and the destiny of others.

All the Light We Cannot See Literary Elements

Genre

Historical fiction

Setting and Context

Germany and France during World War II, years 1939 - 1945, one part in 1974, and one part in 2014.

Narrator and Point of View

Third person omniscient, alternating between Marie-Laure LeBlanc and Werner Pfennig. Other characters' narratives are also shown, such as those of Sergeant Major von Rumpel, Etienne, Daniel LeBlanc, Jutta Pfennig, and Claude Levitte.

Tone and Mood

The mood is a mix of the magic of discovery, the fear of those in power / fear of destruction, and the warmth of love pervading all.

Protagonist and Antagonist

The protagonists are Marie-Laure LeBlanc and Werner Pfennig. The antagonists are von Rumpel, the war, and the Third Reich

Major Conflict

Werner's ethical dilemma in being part of the Nazi regime, as well as his more physical need to escape from the cellar; Marie-Laure's safety in carrying out her duties in the resistance, while also unknowingly keeping the Sea of Flames in her possession, and her need to stay safe from von Rumpel.

Climax

When Saint-Malo is bombed and the protagonists are trapped: Werner, trapped in the basement, with no way to get out, listening to Marie-Laure read on the radio, while she is trapped in the attic hiding the Sea of Flames from von Rumpel.

Foreshadowing

In Chapter 46, von Rumpel notes that a slight swelling troubles his groin, foreshadowing the cancer that later appears in his body and is described in detail in Chapter 62, as the city of Saint Malo burns.

Understatement

In Chapter 171, when Jutta visits Saint-Malo and sees a plaque for the French who died there, she thinks, "There are no plaques for the Germans who died here." This is an understatement because it points indirectly to the severe atrocities that the Germans committed.

"Volkheimer tucks the child's foot gently back inside the closet. 'There's no radio here,' he says, and shuts the door" (Ch 118). This is an understatement because Volkheimer and the rest of the unit already knows there is not a radio there; rather, there is a dead child, and this completely horrifies them.

Allusions

Hades (ch 114): When Werner thinks of the entropy that the Nazis are supposedly trying to weed out of their system, he comes to realize that entropy still prevails, and all the locations that the Nazis have dominated seem as bad as Hades. Hades, the god of the underworld in Greek mythology, was the keeper of the dead; thus it seems to Werner that all of the places the Nazis have touched are full of the dead.

Jules Verne: referenced directly throughout the book, Jules Verne represents a sense of adventure, imagination through story-telling, and scientific discovery.

The Bible: Etienne thinks of the Old Testament's plague of the locusts in Part 1 when he sees the bombs being dropped on Saint-Malo; the bombs, thus, seem to him like a punishment from God. The Bible is again referenced by Jules Verne in the last line of the book Twenty Thousand Leagues Under the Sea, where a quote from Ecclesiastes presents a question about the limits of the human wisdom.

Imagery

One of the most intoxicating images in the book is that of the Sea of Flames, which is cast as a magical diamond of a blue color, with red barely visible on the inside. This diamond feels hot to the touch to Marie-Laure, whereas it feels cold to Daniel LeBlanc; it seems to hold a power that no one can explain.

Paradox

"It floats in a clear liquid inside the skull, never in the light. And yet the world it constructs in the mind is full of light "(Ch 18). This paradox is one of the things "The Professor" says on his radio show. Science, in the context of the book, often takes the form of apparent paradoxes; this is part of what makes science magical for Werner and for Marie-Laure.

Parallelism

"You will become like a waterfall, a volley of bullets—you will all surge in the same direction at the same pace toward the same cause. You will forgo comforts; you will live by duty alone. You will eat country and breathe nation" (ch 45). This is the speech the boys receive upon arriving to Schulpforta. The construction of the sentences parallels what is being said: they have a cadence to them that makes them repetitive and almost catchy, thus serving their purpose of being a memorable ideology the boys can follow.

Metonymy and Synecdoche

Synechdoche: "From your neighborhood," the official says, "from your soil, comes the might of our nation. Steel, coal, coke. Berlin, Frankfurt, Munich—they do not exist without this place. You supply the foundation of the new order, the bullets in its guns, the armor on its tanks" (ch 16). the words here are used to drive home the idea that the coal of the nation embodies all of these forces. Thus the coal of the nation represents all of these things: the might, the bullets, and the armor.

Metonymy: "Marie-Laure looks up from her book and believes she can smell gasoline under the wind. As if a great river of machinery is steaming slowly, irrevocably, toward her" (ch 23). The machinery is more than just the literal tanks and weapons; it is the machinery of Nationalism and war.

Personification

In the climax of the novel, the fire in Saint Malo is personified. The flames that take over Saint Malo have life: “Flames scamper up walls” (Chapter 32).
In Chapter 59, "The drain moans; the cluttered house crowds in close" as Marie-Laure's father prepares to leave to go back to Paris without her, and the house conveys the pain and the fear she feels.
In Chapter 170, when Jutta is trying to contain the emotions that come back to her looking at Werner's things, "Memories cartwheel out of her head and tumble across the floor."

All the Light We Cannot See Links

The rape of Berlin

http://www.bbc.com/news/magazine-32529679

This article explains the disturbing and not often discussed history of Soviet soldiers raping German women at the end of the war, as well as the history of Germans raping Soviet women.

All the Light We Cannot See: Top Travel Destinations from the Novel

http://www.autoeurope.com/blog/destination-spotlight/all-the-light-we-cannot-see-top-travel-destinations-from-the-novel

A review of the destinations shown in the model, a description of their historical significance in the novel, and their present-day status.

On Blindness and the Portrayal of Marie-Laure in All the Light We Cannot See

http://the-toast.net/2016/03/23/on-blindness-and-the-portrayal-of-marie-laure-in-all-the-light-we-cannot-see/

A valuable opinion piece on the inaccuracy of the depiction of blindness in the novel, written by a blind woman.

REVEALED: The tragedy of the Nazi child soldiers rounded up from school

http://www.express.co.uk/news/world/469496/Grim-fate-of-Nazi-child-soldiers-rounded-up-from-school-revealed-in-new-book

Information on the child soldiers used by the Third Reich in World War II.

The Burning of Saint Malo, by Philip Beck

http://www.ihr.org/jhr/v02/v02p301_beck.html

The source from which one of the novel's epigraphs was pulled. This piece tells the history of why Saint-Malo was targeted for bombing, and what was lost in the fires. Originally published in *The Journal of Historical Review*, Winter 1981 (Vol. 2, No. 4), pages 301-304.

All the Light We Cannot See Essay Questions

1. **Consider the structure and the movement in the short chapters, going back and forth through time. "The movement happens on both on a small scale within individual moments, but also on a bigger scale across the entire book" (Smith). Discuss the role time plays in the book.**

   Doerr uses the movement through time to create dramatic suspense in the novel. He also uses it as a way to set the scene and context of a historical fiction where the outcome of the war and the historical event is already known: the suspense is mostly related to the changes within the characters; thus the movement through time allows Doerr to develop Werner's character into one that would save Marie-Laure. The movement also provides space for the reader emotionally, distancing the reader from hard-to-read passages about the atrocities committed in war.

2. **Look again at the two epigraphs:**

   "In August 1944 the historic walled city of Saint-Malo, the brightest jewel of the Emerald Coast of Brittany, France, was almost totally destroyed by fire. . . . Of the 865 buildings within the walls, only 182 remained standing and all were damaged to some degree."—Philip Beck

   "It would not have been possible for us to take power or to use it in the ways we have without the radio."—Joseph Goebbels

   What is the significance of these quotes in the context of the novel?

   The epigraphs touch on two topics: the bombing that occurred in Saint-Malo at the end of WWII, and radio transmissions as used by the Nazis to disseminate propaganda. The first quote, by historian Philip Beck, sets the historical scene of the book, alerting the reader that the novel is set in a time period in which known events occurred. The bombing and destruction of Saint-Malo is woven throughout the novel, and is the setting of the climax of the plot as well. The quote by Goebbels, the Nazi Minister of Propaganda, demonstrates how radio was used as a tool to disseminate propaganda for the Third Reich. Radio plays an important role in the development of the theme of nationalism in the novel; first, with Werner and Jutta's discovery of a radio, where they begin to catch some of the broadcasts of propaganda aimed at children; and later, Werner's expertise in radio engineering wins him a position at an elite school, which in turn leads him to a specialized position in the Wehrmacht fighting.

3. **"Open your eyes and see what you can with them before they close forever" (Chapters 18, 30, 82, 134) is a phrase that appears to Werner repeatedly throughout the book; what is its significance in the novel? What is the relationship between this quote and Madame Manec's question: "Don't you want to be alive before you die?" (Chapters 84 & 144.)**

   This phrase resurfaces for Werner throughout the novel in the theme of memory: it is a comfort to remember those words, which he first heard as a child from his beloved radio with his sister. At that time, the phrase opened his eyes to the magic of science and technology, inspiring him to explore and discover that which fascinated him. Later, the phrase changes meaning for him, as it comes up when he is closing his eyes to the violence around him; he must then open his eyes to the kindness he can participate in, against the odds. Ironically, it was Etienne who wrote that line, and yet, he has not left his home in over 20 years out of fear. Madame Manec's question thus is challenging Etienne years later to return to that place of curiosity and human connection. Etienne's character also progresses in this way: he is able to live a little and open his eyes again by first participating in the resistance, and then later by traveling with Marie-Laure.

4. **Blindness and imagery of the senses form a large part of Marie-Laure's narrative. Think of this sentence: "To shut your eyes is to guess nothing of blindness" (Chapter 127). What is demonstrated to the reader through Marie-Laure's blindness?**

   Marie-Laure's blindness allows her the skill of feeling/hearing/smelling/sensing in some better way than other people. In that way, her blindness is framed as an ironic ability to see more than others. Her blindness is also a tool to allow for sensory imagery outside of what is usually described in imagery, the word itself implying something seen—an image. With Marie-Laure the reader gets to also experience smell, touch, sounds, memories, and imagination associated with these things.

5. **The motif of radio transmission is extremely important in the story and the time period. How does radio help move the plot forward, and how does the meaning of radio change throughout the course of the novel?**

   Radio begins as an exciting experiment in discovery of science and technology for Werner. However, as the radio is used more and more as a tool of German nationalism, Werner succumbs to that version of radio, agreeing to help Dr. Hauptmann with his radio transmitter and transceiver triangle calculations. In a parallel structure, from the other side of the story, radio is initially used by Etienne and by Marie-Laure as a way of hearing news and discovering things from around the world; after it is forbidden, their radio transmitter is also used as a method of resistance against German rule.

These two opposing forces of radio come together at the end, rediscovering the original importance of radio for the characters—connecting people, entertaining, and discovering information—in the communication between Marie-Laure's story telling and Werner's listening in the cellar.

6. **Anthony Doerr has been criticized for the absence of the Jewish side of the World War II story in his novel. Yet, the novel has also won great critical acclaim for its ability to tell a tender story of two children impacted by war. How would you flesh out arguments for both of these perspectives? Which do you think is a more accurate representation of the novel, and why?**

   Doerr's novel is enticing partially because it is so well crafted and suspenseful in the structure and the momentum, and partially also because it is a different view on World War II narrative than the one that is often told. While the story does not entirely ignore the mistreatment of Jewish people by the Germans, it does not put it in the spotlight. This side of the criticism asks whether it is ethical to ignore the Holocaust and all the atrocities that occurred, and instead to focus on a character that is a Nazi, thereby giving very little voice to the victims of the story. However, Doerr's narrative does expand the view of who was impacted by the war: the children in these countries, who had few options presented to them, and made choices out of survival. He highlighted this concept of humanism, strung throughout the novel as a theme of choices that humans can make toward their own destiny; in the end, the narrative makes clear that Germany as a whole made the wrong choice, and the surviving German characters are condemned to their guilt and shame at having been a part of that. Thus the novel does not glorify the Nazis, nor does it recount the horrors of the Holocaust, yet it doesn't paint its characters all as monsters who supported the Nazi regime: its conclusion is more nuanced, residing in the trauma and pain felt by people who participated, marginally or actively, in its unforgettable atrocities.

7. **Why do you think Doerr continued the narrative beyond the wartime period to 1974, and then, at the very end, jumped to 2014? What effect does this achieve for the reader?**

   Because of the historical fiction of the story, the ending of the war is not a surprise in the plot: the plot is instead carried by its characters. By showing us the aftermath of the war in 1974 and how it has damaged or changed the characters in many ways, Doerr goes beyond the context of the war, and of the fairy tale like concepts captured within, and brings a sense of realism to the damage and lasting effects war has on people and on countries.

8. **Take another look at the chapter headings, and their relationship to the content of the chapter, as well as to other chapters—for example, there are two chapters entitled "Leaflets," and there are three chapters with the title "Weakest," and later three entitled "Music." Discuss the use of these chapter headings in the structuring of the plot and the story.**

   These chapter headings often use words from within previous chapters, thus continuing the movement of time for the story, and developing on phrases heard earlier in the novel. For example, the phrase, "Good Evening, or *Heil* Hitler if You Prefer," is said in Chapter 16, and reappears as the title of Chapter 26, when the nationalism in Germany is increasing and Werner begins to feel the ever-expanding machine of Germany. Also, the repeated chapter headings with the title 'Weakest' start with a general story about the first exercise that the boys do to extract the weakest, then zooms in during the next 'Weakest' chapter to show how this exercise impacted Werner when he saw it occurring to Frederick, and finally in the last 'Weakest' chapter we see the climax of the subplot of Frederick's bullying, when he is absent one morning and Werner is confronted once more with the reality of the cruelty that is happening at Schulpforta.

9. **Discuss the use of Jules Verne's *Twenty Thousand Leagues Under the Sea* in the text: what is the relationship between that narrative, those characters, and *All the Light We Cannot See?***

   Unlike *Twenty Thousand Leagues Under the Sea*, there is not much left to question at the end of *All the Light We Cannot See*. Yet there are other important parallels in between the plots and characters that help to move along the plot of Marie-Laure's, and later Werner's, narratives. One parallel is that of Marie-Laure's life in Paris being interrupted: she had to leave the second half of her book there in Paris, and was thus not able to finish the story for many years. After Marie-Laure receives a new copy of the book, she reads a part where Captain Nemo is suspected to be carrying out a secret mission, and this is part of what leads her to realize her father had hidden the Sea of Flames in the model of Saint-Malo. Finally, the excitement and magic and imagination of the story of *Twenty Thousand Leagues* is part of what saves Marie-Laure, because by reading it on the radio, she is able to reach Werner.

All the Light We Cannot See Quizzes

1. **What does Marie-Laure's father do when she goes blind?**

   A. Patiently creates tools, such as a model of their neighborhood, to help Marie-Laure navigate her blindness
   B. Hires an assistant to help her navigate her blindness
   C. Tells the neighbors they are cursed and gets mad when Marie-Laure knocks things over
   D. Gives up and just sits quietly by Marie-Laure's bed

2. **Marie-Laure's father's actions after she becomes blind demonstrate which of these themes:**

   A. Nationalism and humanism
   B. Familial love and nationalism
   C. Humanism and imagination
   D. Imagination and familial love

3. **Which comparison is used to describe cannon in Saint Malo?**

   A. A metaphor compares way the men treat the canon with the respect and admiration the Nazis feel for Hitler
   B. The cannon's power is compared to the power of the radio
   C. The cannon's stinging power is compared to that of a Queen Bee
   D. The cannon is compared to a Queen bee, in the manner in which she is respected by the men using her, who are compared to worker bees

4. **Where is Etienne during the bombing of Saint-Malo?**

   A. Paris
   B. Fort National
   C. Number 4 rue Vauborel
   D. The Chateau

5. **What kind of literary element is used in the following quote: "You will become like a waterfall, a volley of bullets—you will all surge in the same direction at the same pace toward the same cause. You will forgo comforts; you will live by duty alone. You will eat country and breathe nation."**

   A. All are correct
   B. Paraelllism
   C. Metaphor
   D. Synecdoche

6. **What does Marie-Laure count on the streets in order to find her way through the cities she lives in?**
   A. Storm drains
   B. Snails
   C. Trash cans
   D. Doors

7. **What is objects fill Marie-Laure's room in Paris?**
   A. Keys
   B. Pinecones
   C. Seashells
   D. All of these answers are correct

8. **Werner and his sister often use which vehicle to explore?**
   A. A wagon
   B. Riding the local bus
   C. None, they do not often leave their home
   D. A boat they made

9. **Werner's talent for engineering and science is recognized by:**
   A. Herr Seidler
   B. Jutta
   C. Dr. Hauptmann
   D. All of these characters

10. **Which of the answers best describes the themes highlighted in Werner's relationship with Jutta, and Marie-Laure's relationship with her father?**
    A. Imagination and familial love
    B. Imagination and nationalism
    C. Science and technology
    D. Familial love and nationalism

11. **Which of the following is the best example of how humanism portrayed in the novel?**
    A. Madame Manec caters to Etienne's needs because he cannot leave the house
    B. Jutta writes a letter to Werner that is mostly censored
    C. Werner decides to save Marie-Laure
    D. Neumann Two shoots the mother of the girl he killed

12. **Familial love and loyalty is portrayed in the relationships between which characters**
    A. Loving and strict
    B. Strict, authoritarian
    C. Kind, loving, not very strict
    D. Strong willed and opinionated

13. **Which of the following literary devices describes the structure with which the novel begins?**

    A. In media res
    B. Metonymy
    C. Deus Ex Machina
    D. Bildungsroman

14. **Who teaches Marie-Laure about mollusks?**

    A. None of these answers are correct
    B. Dr. Geffard and later, Etienne
    C. Her father, and later Etienne
    D. Her father, and later Dr. Geffard

15. **What does Marie-Laure usually receive on her birthdays**

    A. A wooden model house
    B. A handmade puzzle with a gem inside
    C. A handmade puzzle from her father with a treat inside
    D. A key

16. **What is inside Werner{s childhood notebook?**

    A. His diary
    B. Questions he has, and drawings of inventions
    C. Information on radio transmission
    D. A log of birds he has seen

17. **What do Jutta and Werner call the host of their favorite radio show**

    A. The Professor
    B. Clair de Lune
    C. Henri
    D. All of these answers are correct

18. **Familial love and loyalty is portrayed in the relationships between which characters**

    A. Jutta and Frau Elena
    B. All of the answers are correct
    C. Marie-Laure and Etienne
    D. Volkheimer and Werner

19. **How is Marie-Laure able to learn her way around her neighborhood in Paris?**

    A. She studies the model and goes out with her father to practice
    B. She guides herself solely by smells
    C. She guides herself solely by smells
    D. She never is able to learn the streets

20. **Which theme does Daniel LeBlanc evoke as he tells his daughter what their surrounding are like as they flee Paris**

A. Nationalism
B. Humanism
C. Imagination
D. All of these are correct

21. **What does Daniel LeBlanc believe he carries with him as he flees Paris**

A. A rock that may or may not be the Sea of Flames
B. A puzzle box that may contain a valuable stone
C. The real diamond the Sea of Flames
D. A replica of the Sea of Flames

22. **Who is Joseph Goebbels?**

A. The commandant at Schulpforta
B. The Nazi Minister of Propaganda
C. The Director of the National Fuhrer Museum
D. The Director of the National Museum of Natural History in Paris

23. **What is the purpose of the leaflets?**

A. To warn the civilians in the town to get to safety
B. To strengthen the resistance
C. To announce the arrival of the Americans
D. To warn the Germans to get out of the town safely

24. **What do the Austrian Detachment do while they fire the cannon?**

A. Pray
B. Sing
C. Shout Heil Hitler
D. All of the Answers are Correct

25. **Which allusion occurs as Etienne watches the bombs drop from the sky?**

A. Audubon's descriptions of birds
B. The Locusts in the Old Testament
C. Jules Verne 20,000 Leagues Under the Sea
D. Darwin's theory of survival of the fittest

Quiz 1 Answer Key

1. **(A)** Patiently creates tools, such as a model of their neighborhood, to help Marie-Laure navigate her blindness
2. **(D)** Imagination and familial love
3. **(D)** The cannon is compared to a Queen bee, in the manner in which she is respected by the men using her, who are compared to worker bees
4. **(B)** Fort National
5. **(A)** All are correct
6. **(A)** Storm drains
7. **(B)** Pinecones
8. **(A)** A wagon
9. **(D)** All of these characters
10. **(A)** Imagination and familial love
11. **(C)** Werner decides to save Marie-Laure
12. **(C)** Kind, loving, not very strict
13. **(A)** In media res
14. **(B)** Dr. Geffard and later, Etienne
15. **(C)** A handmade puzzle from her father with a treat inside
16. **(B)** Questions he has, and drawings of inventions
17. **(A)** The Professor
18. **(B)** All of the answers are correct
19. **(A)** She studies the model and goes out with her father to practice
20. **(C)** Imagination
21. **(A)** A rock that may or may not be the Sea of Flames
22. **(B)** The Nazi Minister of Propaganda
23. **(A)** To warn the civilians in the town to get to safety
24. **(B)** Sing
25. **(B)** The Locusts in the Old Testament

All the Light We Cannot See Quizzes

1. **What details does Doerr use to contrast Marie-Laure and Werner´s separate situation in the face of the bombing of Saint-Malo?**
   A. Marie-Laure has a diamond, Werner has his radio
   B. Marie-Laure is in the top of her house, Werner is in the cellar
   C. Marie-Laure has water, Werner forgot water
   D. All of these are correct

2. **What is the setting for Part 1 of the novel?**
   A. Schulpforta and Saint-Malo
   B. Paris and Schulpforta
   C. None of these are correct
   D. Zollverein and Saint-Malo

3. **What is an untermenschen?**
   A. An inferior and unworthy person
   B. A Jew
   C. A small person of diminutive size
   D. An underclassman

4. **What imagery from Heir Seidler's house fascinates Werner**
   A. Frau Seidler's varnished nails and hairless white calves
   B. The large Philco Radio
   C. The dollops of cream on the cake
   D. All of these images

5. **What most motivates Werner to succeed in his entrance exams for the National Political Institute?**
   A. He would like to be physically stronger
   B. His love and admiration for Hitler
   C. He does not want to go to work in the mine
   D. All of these answers are correct

6. **How do Jutta and Werner respond in the face of the German nationalist propaganda?**
   A. Jutta listens to foreign radio to find out what is really happeneing
   B. Werner buries himself in his science books
   C. Werner crushes their radio
   D. All of these answers are correct

7. **How do Jutta and Werner learn French?**
    A. They taught themselves
    B. They learn it in school
    C. Frau Elena speaks it to them growing up
    D. They learn it by listening to the Professor

8. **The radio transmission most embodies which of these literary devices?**
    A. Motif and theme
    B. Motif and metaphor
    C. Motif and simile
    D. Theme and metaphor

9. **Why is Jutta opposed to Werner going to Schulpforta?**
    A. She is worried he will be bullied
    B. She can't go with him
    C. She believes he should follow in their fathers footsteps and be a miner
    D. She thinks he's following what everyone else is doing

10. **Which simile is used to describe the bombs Daniel LeBlanc sees dropping on Paris?**
    A. They are compared to fish in a sea coming in on their prey
    B. They are compared to locusts descending
    C. They are compared to snails being dropped by seagulls
    D. They are compared to demons

11. **Why can't Marie-Laure meet her great-uncle Etienne when she first arrives in Saint-Malo?**
    A. Marie-Laure is too distraught because of leaving Paris
    B. Etienne is in his room and hasn't come out
    C. Marie-Laure doesn't know he's there
    D. Her father says he is too crazy and unstable

12. **Which is an example of dramatic irony?**
    A. The location of the sea of flames is revealed in an early chapter but von Rumpel is not aware of where it is
    B. Etienne has to leave the house to look for Marie-Laure
    C. Werner is trapped in a cellar just like his father got trapped in a mine
    D. The suspense created by the changing of time periods in the parts of the novel

13. **What is one of the reasons Marie-Laure is most excited about living near the ocean in Saint-Malo?**
    A. She thinks it will be a means of escape from France
    B. She's never collected sea snails before
    C. She loves water
    D. She wants to go swimming

14. **Aside from care for the LeBlanc family, what else does Madame Manec do?**
    - A. Bring food to people less fortunate
    - B. Smoke cigarettes
    - C. Organize the resistance amongst her friends
    - D. All of these answers are correct

15. **Which of these figures is most characterized by his commitment to the German Nationalist ideology?**
    - A. The commandant bastian
    - B. Volkheimer
    - C. Werner
    - D. Neumann Two

16. **How does Werner protect Frederick from bullying**
    - A. He helps him with his daily tasks
    - B. He switches bunks
    - C. He fights off the bullies
    - D. All of these answers are correct

17. **What does Dr. Hauptmann habitually say about the calculations he is having Werner do**
    - A. It's just numbers
    - B. It's just science
    - C. It's for the good of our country
    - D. It's just radio

18. **What is the importance of the triangulation calculations Werner is going?**
    - A. Only to find the 3rs point of the triangle
    - B. For a secret project for the fuhrer
    - C. To strengthen the radio
    - D. To discover the locations of partisan broadcasts

19. **Frederick has to leave Schulpforta because:**
    - A. He refused to throw the cold water on the prisoner
    - B. He felt opposed to the mission of Schulpforta
    - C. He was beaten so badly he never recovered
    - D. All of the answers are correct

20. **What does Werner find fascinating about Frederick's life in Berlin?**
    - A. All of the answers are correct
    - B. a Jewess lives in the building
    - C. Frederick wears glasses
    - D. They eat out at a nice bistro

21. **What caused Etienne to go crazy?**
    A. the radio and gas on the brain
    B. studying Science and radio
    C. Witnessing the death of his brother, and gas on the brain
    D. His brother

22. **What is Madame Manec's heaven?**
    A. The beach at Saint Malo
    B. A field of Queen Anne's lace
    C. Angels singing
    D. Gourmet French cuisine

23. **What details does Daniel Leblanc include in his letters about German prison that seem unbelievable to Marie-Laure?**
    A. The meals are gourmet and he has an angel
    B. He has made a lot of friends and the meals are gourmet
    C. He saw a hybrid oak maple tree and he has an angel
    D. The meals are gourmet and he saw a hybrid oak maple tree

24. **Who is Marie-Laure's favorite author**
    A. She can't read, she is blind
    B. Jules Verne
    C. Audubon
    D. Darwin

25. **What will happen to Werner when he turns 15?**
    A. He will have to join the Hitler Youth
    B. He will be considered a man and can leave Children's House
    C. He can go to a boarding school
    D. He will have to go work in the coal mine

Quiz 2 Answer Key

1. **(D)** All of these are correct
2. **(C)** None of these are correct
3. **(A)** An inferior and unworthy person
4. **(D)** All of these images
5. **(C)** He does not want to go to work in the mine
6. **(D)** All of these answers are correct
7. **(C)** Frau Elena speaks it to them growing up
8. **(A)** Motif and theme
9. **(D)** She thinks he's following what everyone else is doing
10. **(A)** They are compared to fish in a sea coming in on their prey
11. **(B)** Etienne is in his room and hasn't come out
12. **(A)** The location of the sea of flames is revealed in an early chapter but von Rumpel is not aware of where it is
13. **(B)** She's never collected sea snails before
14. **(D)** All of these answers are correct
15. **(A)** The commandant bastian
16. **(A)** He helps him with his daily tasks
17. **(A)** It's just numbers
18. **(D)** To discover the locations of partisan broadcasts
19. **(C)** He was beaten so badly he never recovered
20. **(A)** All of the answers are correct
21. **(C)** Witnessing the death of his brother, and gas on the brain
22. **(B)** A field of Queen Anne's lace
23. **(D)** The meals are gourmet and he saw a hybrid oak maple tree
24. **(B)** Jules Verne
25. **(D)** He will have to go work in the coal mine

All the Light We Cannot See Quizzes

1. **How do Etienne and Marie-Laure travel the world from inside his study?**
   A. The radio and imagination
   B. imagination and the Davenport
   C. an imaginary Submarine
   D. Darwin's narratives

2. **Why did Etienne broadcast his brother's recordings?**
   A. He doesn't really know
   B. To try and reach his brother
   C. For children
   D. To try and teach Marie-Laure

3. **How many "sea of flames" replicas exist?**
   A. 0
   B. 2
   C. 3
   D. 4

4. **Why is von Rumpel so interested in finding the sea of flames?**
   A. He needs it to cure his cancer
   B. He imagines it as the centerpiece of the fuhrer museum and he also hopes it will save him from jos cancer
   C. He is obsessed with valuable gems
   D. He does it solely for the devotion to he fuhrer

5. **What does von Rumpel consider his most valuable trait**
   A. Patience
   B. His devotion to the fuhrer
   C. His love for his daughters
   D. His talent for gems

6. **What does Madame Manec do for Marie-Laure to bring her out of her depression after her father leaves**
   A. Petitions the ministry for information on Daniel LeBlanc
   B. Makes her gourmet meals
   C. Takes her to the beach
   D. All of these answers are correct

7. **What imagery does Marie-Laure envision for her mother?**
   A. She doesn't see images
   B. A bright white light
   C. multiple colors
   D. A warm loving woman

8. **Where does Marie-Laure go secretly after she picks up the bread?**
   A. To the old kennel
   B. To the hotel of bees
   C. To the attic
   D. All of these are correct

9. **How old is Werner when he is sent into the Wehrmacht?**
   A. 16, but he is told he is 18
   B. He realizes he doesn't know how old he is
   C. 15, but the Wehrmacht is so desperate they don't care
   D. 18, he has been pretending to be 16

10. **What does Volkheimer listen to in the lab when Dr Hauptmann is not around?**
   A. All of the answers are correct
   B. Classical music
   C. The fuhrer
   D. He looks for partisan broadcasts

11. **What is the phrase that Volkheimer says to Werner that is later repeated in the text as a memory?**
   A. What the war does to dreamers
   B. What you could have been
   C. Open your eyes and see with them what you can before they close forever
   D. Who is the weakest?

12. **What is the name of Captain Nemo's submarine?**
   A. Ecclesiastes
   B. Stormy Weather
   C. Whelk
   D. Nautilus

13. **What reanimates Volkheimer to find a way out of the cellar in Saint-Malo?**
   A. Hearing the voice of Marie-Laure
   B. Listening to the story of 20,000 Leagues Under the Sea
   C. Talking to Werner
   D. Hearing the classical music

14. **What does Marie-Laure choose as her pseudonym in the French Resistance?**

A. The Whelk
B. The Blade
C. Captain Nemo
D. The Professor

15. **What imagery does Doerr use to emphasize the contrast between Werner's former setting and Schulpforta?**

A. The strong feeling of nationalism vs the absence of nationalism in Zollverein
B. The phrenology teachings, and Werner´s absence of knowledge on the subject before
C. The lack of women in Schulpforta vs Frau Elena and Jutta
D. The purity of the air and the snow in Schulpforta vs the dusty coal town of Zollverein

16. **What is Volkheimer's nickname amongst the boys of schulpforta?**

A. The Sap
B. The Blade
C. The Giant
D. The Killer

17. **When does Marie-Laure start going outside by herself in Saint-Malo**

A. After her father disappears
B. She never goes outside except to flee the bombings
C. After Madame Manec dies
D. After Etienne disappears

18. **Who is Daniels foil?**

A. Claude Levitte
B. the Fuhror
C. Marie-Laure
D. The Museum Director

19. **Who is the creator of the replica Sea of Flames?**

A. The Museum Director
B. DuPont
C. Daniel LeBlanc
D. Dr. Geffard

20. **What theme is expressed in Jutta's relationship with Frau Elena**

A. Science and Technology
B. Humanism
C. Imagination
D. Familial Love

21. **Which two important topics are highlighted in the epigraph?**
    A. radio and the bombing of Saint Malo
    B. the bombing of Saint-Malo and the fall of Hitler
    C. Radio and Darwin
    D. radio and nazism

22. **What metaphor or simile is used to describe von Rumpel's cancer?**
    A. Loneliness like a disease
    B. A plague of locusts descending
    C. A black tree growing branches
    D. Fish circling in on its prey

23. **Where is the Sea of Flames hidden during the course of the war?**
    A. In Daniel LeBlanc's tool kit
    B. Inside the model house of rue Vauborel number 4
    C. Inside the model in their house in Paris
    D. Inside the museum behind 13 doors

24. **What is the code word that Marie-Laure uses to get the scroll of paper to read on the radio**
    A. The mermaids with bleached hair
    B. The blade
    C. The whelk
    D. An ordinary loaf

25. **What does the sea of flames look like?**
    A. A completely clear and perfect diamond
    B. red, with blue flames throughout
    C. Dark blue all the way through
    D. None of these answers are correct

Quiz 3 Answer Key

1. **(B)** imagination and the Davenport
2. **(B)** To try and reach his brother
3. **(C)** 3
4. **(B)** He imagines it as the centerpiece of the fuhrer museum and he also hopes it will save him from jos cancer
5. **(A)** Patience
6. **(D)** All of these answers are correct
7. **(B)** A bright white light
8. **(A)** To the old kennel
9. **(A)** 16, but he is told he is 18
10. **(B)** Classical music
11. **(B)** What you could have been
12. **(D)** Nautilus
13. **(D)** Hearing the classical music
14. **(A)** The Whelk
15. **(D)** The purity of the air and the snow in Schulpforta vs the dusty coal town of Zollverein
16. **(C)** The Giant
17. **(C)** After Madame Manec dies
18. **(A)** Claude Levitte
19. **(B)** DuPont
20. **(D)** Familial Love
21. **(A)** radio and the bombing of Saint Malo
22. **(C)** A black tree growing branches
23. **(B)** Inside the model house of rue Vauborel number 4
24. **(D)** An ordinary loaf
25. **(D)** None of these answers arc correct

All the Light We Cannot See Quizzes

1. **Which theme is demonstrated most through repetition of phrases throughout the novel?**
   A. Humanism
   B. Nationalism
   C. Memory
   D. Science and technology

2. **How do Werner and Volkheimer escape from the cellar**
   A. Rescuers come and find them
   B. They use one of Volkheimer's grenades
   C. They never get out
   D. They finally find an opening behind the white heads

3. **What is Marie-Laure's favorite food that Madame Manec cans?**
   A. Peaches
   B. Beans
   C. Grapes
   D. Potatoes

4. **What do the leaflets say that are dropped on Saint Malo before the bombing?**
   A. Saint-Malo will be bombed
   B. Urgent message to the inhabitants of this town. Depart immediately to open country
   C. The Americans are coming
   D. Evacuate immediately

5. **What book does Werner see at Etienne's house that most catches his attention?**
   A. Darwin´s writings
   B. The Jules Verne book in braile
   C. The book by Audubon about birds
   D. The Principles of Mechanics

6. **What items of Werner's are returned to Jutta at the end of the novel?**
   A. his childhood notebook
   B. A duffel, a notebook, and the sea of flames
   C. A duffel, a notebook, and a small model house
   D. a letter he wrote to her before he died

7. **What is Volkheimer's profession later in life?**
    A. TV Antenna repairman
    B. Radio repairman
    C. Traveling salesman
    D. Chauffer

8. **What is the song that Werner recognizes on the radio broadcast?**
    A. Nautilus
    B. L'Atunne
    C. He isn't sure of the name, he just knows the tune
    D. Clair de Lune

9. **How does Jutta feel when Volkheimer brings Werner's belongings to her home?**
    A. Grateful that he came so far to drop off the belongings
    B. Upset, she wants him to leave and take the belongings with him
    C. Scared because of Volkheimer's stature
    D. All of these answers are correct

10. **Which two figures appear to Werner in his final hours trapped in the cellar?**
    A. Marie-Laure and Jutta
    B. The Viennese Girl and Marie-Laure
    C. The Viennese girl and Jutta
    D. The Viennese Girl and Frau Schwartzenberger

11. **The title of one chapter is The Final Sentence; this is in reference to:**
    A. The words of Frau Schwartzenberger
    B. The death of the Viennese Girl
    C. The final sentence of Twenty Thousand Leagues Under the Sea
    D. All of these answers are correct

12. **As von Rumpel struggles to find the Sea of Flames, he gets lost in a delirious memory about:**
    A. The look of the white haired soldier he saw outside the bakery
    B. His daughter Veronika
    C. The glory of the fuhrermuseum he will help build
    D. The beauty of the Sea of Flames

13. **Sight and Vision serves as which of the following literary elements:**
    A. Symbol
    B. Theme
    C. Motif
    D. Synecdoche

14. **What does Marie-Laure keep in her laboratory?**

A. Lots of snail shells

B. Pinecones

C. Little model houses

D. Live tanks full of snails

15. **What is Jutta's profession in 1974?**

A. Scientist

B. Algebra teacher

C. Engineer

D. Works in a factory

16. **Why does Jutta say she'd like o go to Saint Malo with her son Max?**

A. She wants Max to learn French

B. She wants to see the ocean

C. She wants a summer vacation

D. All of these answers are correct

17. **What does Volkheimer teach Max to do?**

A. Say Heil Hitler

B. Build a special paper airplane

C. Build a simple radio

D. Use a Mauser rifle

18. **How is Max similar to Werner?**

A. He speaks French and asks a lot of impossible questions

B. He has white hair

C. He loves the Principles of Mechanics

D. He has ears that stick out and asks a lot of impossible questions

19. **What imagery is used when Jutta gives marie-Laure the wooden model of Rue Vauborel number 4?**

A. A warmth inside her

B. Memories tumbling out of her head onto the floor

C. Shining strangely cold

D. A molten hot memory

20. **Which simile is used to describe Volkheimer's life in 1974**

A. he feels his loneliness like a disease

B. He feels the black branches of a tree growing up inside him

C. Guilt like a disease

D. All of these answers are correct

21. **What theme is portrayed by Werner rescuing Marie-Laure?**
   A. Familial love and loyalty
   B. Imagination
   C. Nationalism
   D. Humanism

22. **Which literary elements are portrayed in the reading of Jules Verne on the radio?**
   A. Metonymy and parallelism
   B. Theme of imagination and motif of radio transmission
   C. Theme of memory and parallelism
   D. theme of nationalism, and motif of the whelk

23. **What is Marie-Laure's daughters name?**
   A. Joanna
   B. Ruelle
   C. Helene
   D. Manec

24. **In honor of Dr Geffard, what does Marie Laure do?**
   A. Organize her shells according to size and species
   B. Eat duck
   C. Goes by the name Laurette
   D. Keeps live snails in her office

25. **In the end, Marie Laure thinks of radio waves and their relationship to:**
   A. the memory that technology contains
   B. propaganda and nationalism
   C. Current cell phone waves, and where the souls of the dead might exist
   D. cell phones and the evilness of technology

Quiz 4 Answer Key

1. **(C)** Memory
2. **(B)** They use one of Volkheimer's grenades
3. **(A)** Peaches
4. **(B)** Urgent message to the inhabitants of this town. Depart immediately to open country
5. **(C)** The book by Audubon about birds
6. **(C)** A duffel, a notebook, and a small model house
7. **(A)** TV Antenna repairman
8. **(D)** Clair de Lune
9. **(B)** Upset, she wants him to leave and take the belongings with him
10. **(D)** The Viennese Girl and Frau Schwartzenberger
11. **(D)** All of these answers are correct
12. **(B)** His daughter Veronika
13. **(C)** Motif
14. **(D)** Live tanks full of snails
15. **(B)** Algebra teacher
16. **(D)** All of these answers are correct
17. **(B)** Build a special paper airplane
18. **(D)** He has ears that stick out and asks a lot of impossible questions
19. **(D)** A molten hot memory
20. **(A)** he feels his loneliness like a disease
21. **(D)** Humanism
22. **(B)** Theme of imagination and motif of radio transmission
23. **(C)** Helene
24. **(B)** Eat duck
25. **(C)** Current cell phone waves, and where the souls of the dead might exist

All the Light We Cannot See Bibliography

Rachel Younger, author of ClassicNote. Completed on April 1, 2017, copyright held by GradeSaver.

Updated and revised by Aaron Suduiko May 19, 2017. Copyright held by GradeSaver.

Doerr, Anthony. All the Light We Cannot See. New York, NY: Scribner, 2014.

Den Heyer, K. and Fidyk, A. (2007), CONFIGURING HISTORICAL FACTS THROUGH HISTORICAL FICTION: AGENCY, ART-IN-FACT, AND IMAGINATION AS STEPPING STONES BETWEEN THEN AND NOW. Educational Theory, 57: 141–157. doi:10.1111/j.1741-5446.2007.00249.x

"Anthony Doerr | Writer." 21 March, 2017. <http://www.anthonydoerr.com/>.

Tuck, Kathleen. "Anthony Doerr." Boise State University. 29 December, 2014. 21 March, 2017. <https://news.boisestate.edu/update/2014/12/29/anthony-doerr-2/>.

"Anthony Doerr." Wikipedia. 1 March, 2017. 21 March, 2017. <https://en.wikipedia.org/wiki/Anthony_Doerr>.

Panda, Pooja. "Interview: Antony Doer." Tweed's Magazine of Literature and Art. 21 March, 2017. <http://tweedsmag.org/interview-anthony-doerr/>.

"Definition of Humanism." American Humanist Association. 25 March 2017. <https://americanhumanist.org/what-is-humanism/definition-of-humanism/>.

Green, Dominic. "One-Armed Nazis and Albino Children: The Year's Surprise Bestseller Turns the Holocaust into a Sentimental Mess." The New Republic. 14 January, 2015. 22 March, 2017. <https://newrepublic.com/article/120769/problem-anthony-doerrs-all-light-we-cannot-see>.

"Battle of Moscow." Wikipedia. 25 March, 2017. <https://en.wikipedia.org/wiki/Battle_of_Moscow>.

"Diamond Clarity." Wikipedia. 25 March, 2017. <https://en.wikipedia.org/wiki/Diamond_clarity>.

"Jules Verne." Wikipedia. 26 March 2017. <https://en.wikipedia.org/wiki/Jules_Verne>.

Trueman, CN. "National Political Training Institutes." The History Learning Site. 9 March 2015. 26 March 2017. <http://www.historylearningsite.co.uk/nazi-germany/national-political-training-institutes/>.

Margaronis, Maria . "The Anxiety of Authenticity: Writing Historical Fiction at the End of the Twentieth Century." Hist Workshop J (2008) 65 (1): 138-160. 1 March 2008. 30 March, 2017. <https://academic.oup.com/hwj/article-abstract/65/1/138/640501/The-Anxiety-of-Authenticity-Writing-Historical>.

"How Anthony Doerr Came to Write All the Light We Cannot See." Scribner, Between the Lines. October 2014. 26 March, 2017. <http://www.scribnermagazine.com/2014/10/anthony-doerr-all-the-light-we-cannot-see/>.

"All the Light We Cannot See FAQ." Anthony Press. 1 December, 2013. 30 March, 2017. <http://www.anthonydoerr.com/press/441/>.

"Humanism." Merriam-Webster. 30 March, 2017. <https://www.merriam-webster.com/dictionary/humanism>.

Smith, Nancy. "THE RUMPUS INTERVIEW WITH ANTHONY DOERR." The Rumpus. 28 May, 2014. 23 March, 2017. <http://therumpus.net/2014/05/the-rumpus-interview-with-anthony-doerr/>.

Essay Childhood in All the Light We Cannot See: A Defining Moment

by Anonymous

The chain of dependency is innate within human society. As children develop, their attitudes and behaviors are modeled after their parents. This mutual growth has sustained the relationship between a child and his or her parent. In *All the Light We Cannot See* (hereinafter referred to as "the Novel"), the influence of having and lacking parents is evident in the lives of Marie-Laure LeBlanc and Werner Pfennig, respectively. Despite the absence of Werner's biological parents, the fundamental needs for love and care are upheld by the caregiver of the orphanage, Frau Elena. As proposed by David Suzuki in "Hidden Lessons" (hereinafter referred to as "the Essay"), the natural bond between a child and his or her parent surpasses the integrated relationship between society and its environment. As demonstrated in the Novel, the role of a parent is not bounded by blood; rather, the relationship is nurtured through time and substantive interactions. This bond is evidently present in the development of modern adolescents. Despite the independence that children acquire through age, the Novel and the Essay emphasize on the lasting effects that children experience through the relationship with their parents.

In the Essay, Suzuki stresses the importance of behaving cautiously in front of children. Unconsciously, children are constantly modeling after "the unspoken, negative lessons [that parents] are conveying" (Suzuki 129). Similarly, Werner has prioritized his the importance of his own career due to the disappearance of his father. Through the fear of experiencing the same fate as his father, Werner is desperate to avoid the coal mines. This demonstrates that parental influence can be conveyed through direct and indirect interactions. It should be emphasized that the influence of his father persists beyond his physical presence. Partially, the relationship has been shaped by a reactionary progression. That is, the relationship develops based on how each party reacts to the other. Unfortunately, this issue is neglected in the Essay due to its emphasis on parental influence over mutual influence. Since Suzuki is targeting specifically young children and their parents, the Essay is not considerate of the independence that older children gain. Through the development of independence, their thoughts become more personal. Likewise, Werner may have grew up without his biological parents, but his limited experience with them creates a foundation for his mindset. As he becomes more independent, Werner adapts according to his relationship with his father rather than abandoning his past. The adaptive characteristic of a parent-child relationship has allowed for a mutual yet independent development for both parties.

Although Werner had lost his biological parents, the role has been fulfilled by Frau Elena after being sent to an orphanage. Throughout Werner's life, he has always been inspired by the words of Frau Elena. Despite the lack of consanguinity, her influence on Werner is substantial. While Suzuki addresses mainly parents, he starts the Essay with the recognition of "a world [that is] conceived, shaped, and dominated by people" (Suzuki 127). This statement implies that human societies are driven through the interactions between individuals. Therefore, the group dynamic of humanity has given substantive qualities to every relationship that each individual partakes in. Due to the unique characteristics of these relationships, it is appropriate to consider Frau Elena to be a parent to Werner, because guardians and foster parents can adequately fulfill the fundamental role that a parent serves. As a matter of fact, Werner recognizes that Frau Elena is "as close to a mother as he will ever have" (Doerr 86). The emotional dependency that Werner feels is similar to the innate dependency that a child would feel with his or her biological parent. Ultimately, these physical and emotional dependencies create the influential effects that parents and guardians pertain.

Due to the immense influence that parents have, Suzuki reminds his readers to think conscientiously and act accordingly. In the Essay, there is an overt emphasis on being prudent and aware of the future consequences of their actions. However, the parents from the Novel seldom reflect on their actions. Marie-Laure's father, Daniel, reflects on his choices only before his departure from her. In retrospect, there is always "a fear that he is no good as a father" (Doerr 188). Since it can be difficult to envision the errors of one's actions, people are often deterred from acting beyond intuition. As Suzuki explains, the generational continuation of ignorance has threatened the environment and the potential survival of humanity. That is, the ideas of one generation can be easily passed onto the next if parents do not reflect on the merit of their own decisions. Due to conformity, the parent-child relationship for one family can be influenced by mainstream society. As demonstrated in the Novel, Daniel may be able to question his actions in retrospect, but there is still an uncertainty from the existing circumstances. Due to the war and his duty in protecting the Sea of Flames, Daniel is forced to abandon his duty of caring for Marie-Laure over the duty of his job. Nevertheless, Daniel still acknowledges his responsibility in protecting Marie-Laure by entrusting it to Etienne, her great-uncle. Similarly, this duty of care is promoted in the Essay as a means of reminding parents that environmental pollution "has violated their home" (Suzuki 129). By making environmental issues more personal, Suzuki is able to convey his arguments to his readers. One of the main concerns about climate change is the sustainability of future generations. Although it is difficult for parents to consistently be prudent of their actions, the underlying principle of protection has guided the decision-making in a parent-child relationship.

However, the principle of protection has conflicted with the many aspirations of each party. This is evident in the relationship between Werner and Frau Elena. While they want the best for each other, they still want to fulfill their personal dreams and commitments. The difference is that Frau Elena wishes to continue caring for Werner, yet he wishes to continue his studies. Interestingly, Werner's aspirations have been strongly motivated by Frau Elena's encouragement. In fact, Suzuki suggests that the natural aspirations of children can be completely altered through parental involvement. Although "all scientists were fascinated with nature as children," many of them are changed by the "hidden lessons" that parents give (Suzuki 128 - 129). Likewise, the disappearance of Werner's father has also influenced his aspirations. Rather than inspiring Werner, his father indirectly warns him of what to avoid. Due to the mutual yet independent characteristic of the parent-child relationship, each party has his or her own interpretation of the relationship and how to contribute to it. While Werner's father is no longer with him, Werner still interprets his view of reality through the memories of their past relationship. Due to a mutual influence on each other, personal aspirations merge into common goals and vice versa. Although Frau Elena was reluctant to let Werner leave, it is ultimately agreed that it is the most beneficial toward Werner's future. Again, the principle of protection gives priority to the long-term happiness of the child. The process of compromise has shaped the aspirations of each party while maintaining satisfaction between them. By finally acknowledging Werner as being self-sufficient, Frau Elena accepts that she has fulfilled her duty of care for Werner. Effectively, the adaptation of personal aspirations helps settle the relationship to a state of mutual happiness.

However, mutual happiness is not eternal, and when there is a loss thereof, a desire for status quo is created. Since Marie-Laure and Daniel were happy with their life in Paris, they are shocked by the fact that they are fleeing from it. During their time in Paris, Marie-Laure "presume[s] she would live with her father in Paris for the rest of her life"; thus, she does not aspire for anything more (Doerr 72). It is until they fled Paris that they aspire for a status quo in their life. This suggests that mutual happiness allows for personal happiness, and if removed, their personal aspirations become a demand for nostalgia. To the child, the relationship outlines an ideal standard of life. When Werner lost his father, he tries to convinces himself that eventually his "father might come shuffling out of the elevators" (Doerr 86). Mainly, Werner is trying to help his sister, Jutta, accepts that the unfortunate had happened. Both Werner and Jutta have trouble with accepting a reality without their biological family. Likewise, Marie-Laure is in despair from the disappearance of Daniel. In both situations, the loss of a parent has a negative effect on the child. However, an important stage of the parent-child relationship is accepting the reality of death. Although death is part of the cycle, it does not signify any loss in the value of the relationship nor the amount of influence that it has had on the child. Instead, these obstacles evoke each party to appreciate and to long for the pleasant memories from their relationship.

While Suzuki emphasizes on the negative influence of parental involvement, the Novel highlights the encouraging and inspirational influence that parents provide. As a matter of fact, Suzuki acknowledges that the "efforts to teach children to love and respect other life forms are priceless" (Suzuki 129). That is, negative behaviors can only be avoided and corrected through positive parental involvement. There is little doubt about the impact that parenting can have, but there is a strong debate about which parenting style is the most effective. Terms such as "helicopter" and "free-range" parenting are used to classify the level of parental involvement. Helicopter parenting is described as being over-protective; while, free-range parenting is described as being neglectful (Sauriol). Arguably, Marie-Laure is raised by an helicopter parent and Werner is raised by a free-range parent. According to Suzuki, it is not about the level of parental involvement; instead, it is the implications that are conveyed to the child. As stated by Sauriol, balance is the most important part in parenting. While Daniel is a protective father, Marie-Laure is more confident and independent than what is suggested by stereotypical media. Naturally, the question of parenting style is based on compromise between the child and his or her parent. In terms of Marie-Laure, it is natural for Daniel to be concerned due to her blindness. Likewise, Marie-Laure accepts and appreciates the level of care that is provided to her. In accordance to the principle of protection, all forms of parenting are in the best interest of the child. The question lies on whether the parent has an healthy interpretation of what is beneficial for the child.

Nevertheless, most modern families maintain a nurturing and pleasant parent-child relationship. In fact, modern adolescents are delaying their departure from the parental home. It implies that they have a stronger attachment and dependency than preceding generations. According to the 2011 Census of Population, 42.3% of those who are aged 20 to 29 remain or return to the parental home. In comparison, the statistics from 1991 and 1981 were 32.1% and 26.9%, respectively. This trend in modern society provides a mutual benefit to the parent and the child. That is, the child gains from the emotional and financial support that are provided by the parent; while, the parent gains from the contributions that are made to the household (Milan and Bohnert). Similar to the attitude of Marie-Laure, modern adolescents are more willing to live with their parents. It does not necessarily mean that modern adolescents are any less independent; rather, they are becoming more defined by their parent-child relationship.

Since parents are the primary agent of socialization, moral principles are learned from childhood through family interactions. During Werner's moral dilemmas, he imagines "his mother and father ... watching him through the rattling window to see what he would do" (Doerr 251). The implication is that personal morals are ultimately a manifestation of parental ideals. When Werner was attending the National Political Institute of Education, his personal morals persist despite the teachings from the school. This justifies the willingness to stay in the parental home, because children are already accustomed to the family in which they grew up in. Although parents may conform to society, children are primarily influenced by their parents instead of the society in general.

Throughout the lives of children, experience shapes the various aspects of their personalities. As warned by Suzuki, parental involvement may unconsciously tarnish the natural progression of their growth. However, the parent-child relationship is an essential part of every child's life. Doerr effectively exhibits that the fundamental element of love is innate within humanity as the parent-child relationship transcends consanguinity. In modern society, the natural bond within families are ever growing as adolescents delay their transition into full independence. While children will grow to be discreet individuals, their personalities shall be a manifestation of the qualities that are modeled from the substantive interactions with their parents. As the issue of child development lies in the hands of parents, every moment is crucial to the potential of the future generations.

Works Cited

Doerr, Anthony. *All the Light We Cannot See: A Novel.* New York: Scribner, 2014. Print.

Milan, Anne, and Nora Bohnert. "Living Arrangements of Young Adults Aged 20 to 29." *Statistics Canada.* Canada.ca, 22 Dec. 2015. Web. 02 May 2016. <https://www12.statcan.gc.ca/census-recensement/2011/as-sa/98-312-x/98-312-x2011003_3-eng.cfm>.

Sauriol, Kerry. "What's Between Helicopter and Free-Range Parenting? Common Sense." *CBC Parents.* CBC/Radio-Canada, 30 May 2013. Web. 02 May 2016. <http://www.cbc.ca/parents/learning/view/my_free-range_parenting_ways>.

Suzuki, David. "Hidden Lessons." *The Act of Writing: Canadian Essays for Composition.* 6th ed. Conrad, Ronald. Toronto: McGraw-Hill Ryerson, 2003. Print.

Essay The Light We Must See

by Anonymous

Through All The Light We Cannot See, Anthony Doerr creates a world in which two invariably different individuals connect to one another by way of fate and personal faults. Werner's shortcomings - or his inability to visualize his hope - are aligned with Marie-Laure's lack of sight. Werner and Marie-Laure are forced - in their own realities and together, upon meeting one another - to understand that the world is far from good. That does not, however, mean they can submit to the bad (Nazism, for Werner; sadness, for Marie-Laure). They come to the realization that one must, "Open your eyes and see what you can with them before they close forever" (Doerr, 310), adding a tragic dash of situational irony in light of Marie-Laure's lack of ability to, physically, do precisely that. All The Light We Cannot See, through this connection, becomes a search for light in the tunnel of life, and the presence or lack of sight in the novel provide symbols for hope and the obstacles individuals encounter during that search.

The obstacles Marie-Laure and Werner encounter aim to dissuade them from seeing (physically and metaphorically), but they are ultimately able to overcome those obstacles by acknowledging the errors of their ways and opening their eyes to hope - to light - in life. Marie-Laure's abilities are obviously hindered by her physical blindness, but her obstacles stand deeper; they begin as a battle against hopelessness and evolve to a battle against the evil of the Nazi cause, a battle for her life. Marie-Laure's Father instills in her a deep self-sufficiency and intelligence that allows her hope - her light, her sight - to grow, as he works with her to see the city (through his models) in spite of her disability. Her father's diligent and careful teachings are what gives Marie-Laure the moral standard and courage to help her uncle and what allows Marie-Laure's hope to thrive. Werner, in his parallel, is forced to work in a Hitler Youth programme on behalf of the Nazi cause. He must turn passion for science and radio that he once used to find music and the philosophical words of a Frenchman - he once used for good - into a tool to find and eliminate those against the Nazi cause. He must to facilitate the deaths of people who want only the same basic humanities he craved as a young, orphan boy; safety, happiness, care. His duty to the Nazi cause and fear of potential repercussions - if he were to demur - destroy his moral and hurt his integrity, stealing his light, and clouding his sight of hope. It is through fulfilling his baneful duties that Werner discovers Marie-Laure; Marie-Laure's Uncle Etienne had radio broadcasts in the interest of the 'rebel cause'. (Uncle Etienne, in a perfectly wholesome literary circle, is the same Frenchman who Werner had listened to on his radio and idolized as a child.) Werner, in meeting Marie-Laure - in seeing her for the first time - is reminded of the Werner he wants to be; the Werner who Jutta, his sister, begged him to remain; the Werner he knew he was, at heart. He decides he will not stand by and assist in the murder of undeserving people for the sake of a supposed cause. Werner saves Marie-Laure and Etienne, crediting Marie-Laure as the catalyst that brings light back to him, letting him open his eyes and allowing him to see his hope.

Werner comes to understand the reality he could have had, instead of the misery he endured with the Nazis, before meeting Marie-Laure, and is able to continue the rest of his life for the betterment of his moral stability and correction of his malfeasance; he needed a blind woman to help him see. He finally stands up for who he is and what he believes by helping Marie-Laure in the way he could not help himself or Jutta growing up, and how he could not help the people whose deaths he caused: by protecting her. As he briefly tells Jutta in the latter half of the book, he is a changed man, he knows he must stand up to Von Rumpel and the cause, he sees now. The time Werner and Marie-Laure share is not long, but nevertheless allows them to harbor a deep care for each other; Werner ultimately loses his life protecting her - as he took the stone which, provided a fantastical scapegoat for Marie-Laure's misfortunes - in doing so, running from his Nazi obligations, and protecting himself.

The biggest troubles of Werner and Marie-Laure stem from their inability to see hope, from their closed eyes. Marie-Laure's main personal struggles surface in the primary half of the book, as she learns to cope with her developing blindness, the loss of her father, the rise of Nazism, and her spatial ignorance upon leaving Paris. She is tempted, by hopelessness, to simply give up. But through the care and keeping of her father, Marie-Laure is able to develop her own persuasion of sight - to bear witness to the good in life, like the music and literature she broadcasts - which compensates her literal infirmity to visualize. She uses her sight to help the rebel cause in tandem with Etienne, and instill faith and hope (her own forms of sight) in characters like Madame Manec. Werner, in a similarly formatted escapade, begins as an orphaned underdog, eventually having the one thing he loves (science - his radio) used against him. In the wake of carrying out what the Nazi cause labels 'duties' - and Werner deems immoral, evil acts - Werner loses the sight that Marie-Laure possesses; the ability to see hope and light. He needs a task, the task of protecting Marie-Laure, to reiterate his personal beliefs and allow him to come into the visible, hopeful light, before he loses his life. Marie-Laure is able to overcome her blindness with moral vision, and Werner is able to move past his own blindness - hopelessness - thanks to Marie-Laure's sight.

ClassicNotes

GradeSaver™

Getting you the grade since 1999™

Other ClassicNotes from GradeSaver™

Politics and the English Language
Pope's Poems and Prose
Portrait of the Artist as a Young Man
Pride and Prejudice
Private Memoirs and Confessions of a Justified Sinner
Prometheus Bound
Psycho
Pudd'nhead Wilson
Purple Hibiscus
Pygmalion
Rabbit, Run
Rashomon
Ray Bradbury: Short Stories
Reached
Reading Lolita in Tehran
Rear Window
Rebecca
Reflections on Gandhi
Regeneration
Return of the Native
Rhinoceros
Richard II
Richard III
Riders to the Sea
Rip Van Winkle and Other Stories
Robert Browning: Poems
Robert Frost: Poems
Robinson Crusoe
Roll of Thunder, Hear My Cry
Roman Fever and Other Stories
Romeo and Juliet
Roots
Rosencrantz and Guildenstern Are Dead
Rudyard Kipling: Poems
Salome
Salvage the Bones
Schindler's List
Season of Migration to the North
Second Treatise of Government
Secret Sharer
Self Reliance and Other Essays
Sense and Sensibility
Shakespeare's Sonnets
Shantaram
She Stoops to Conquer

ClassicNotes

GradeSaver™

Getting you the grade since 1999™

Other ClassicNotes from GradeSaver™

The Alchemist (Jonson)
The Ambassadors
The American
The Analects of Confucius
The Arabian Nights: One Thousand and One Nights
The Autobiography of an Ex-Colored Man
The Autobiography of Benjamin Franklin
The Awakening
The Bacchae
The Bean Trees
The Beggar's Opera
The Bell Jar
The Bet
The BFG
The Birthday Party
The Blithedale Romance
The Bloody Chamber
The Bonfire of the Vanities
The Book of Daniel
The Book of the Duchess and Other Poems
The Book Thief
The Boy in the Striped Pajamas
The Brief Wondrous Life of Oscar Wao
The Brothers Karamazov
The Burning Plain and Other Stories
The Canterbury Tales
The Caretaker
The Castle of Otranto
The Catcher in the Rye
The Caucasian Chalk Circle
The Cherry Orchard
The Children's Hour
The Chocolate War
The Chosen
The Chrysalids
The Chrysanthemums
The Circle
The Collector
The Color of Water
The Color Purple
The Consolation of Philosophy
The Coquette
The Count of Monte Cristo

ClassicNotes

Getting you the grade since 1999™

Other ClassicNotes from GradeSaver™

The Grapes of Wrath
The Great Gatsby
The Guest
The Handmaid's Tale
The Heart of the Matter
The Help
The Hiding Place
The History Boys
The History of Rasselas: Prince of Abissinia
The History of Tom Jones, a Foundling
The Hobbit
The Homecoming
The Hot Zone
The Hound of the Baskervilles
The House of Bernarda Alba
The House of the Seven Gables
The House of the Spirits
The Hunger Games
The Idea of Order at Key West
The Importance of Being Earnest
The Infinite Sea
The Interlopers
Their Eyes Were Watching God
The Island of Dr. Moreau
The Jew of Malta
The Joy Luck Club
The Jungle
The Kill Order
The Kite Runner
The Lais of Marie de France
The Legend of Sleepy Hollow
The Life of Olaudah Equiano
The Lightning Thief
The Lion and the Jewel
The Lion, the Witch and the Wardrobe
The Lone Ranger and Tonto Fistfight in Heaven
The Lord of the Rings: The Fellowship of the Ring
The Lord of the Rings: The Return of the King
The Lord of the Rings: The Two Towers

ClassicNotes

Getting you the grade since 1999™

Other ClassicNotes from GradeSaver™

The Portrait of a Lady
The Praise of Folly
The Prince
The Professor's House
The Quiet American
The Ramayana
The Real Inspector Hound
The Real Life of Sebastian Knight
The Red Badge of Courage
The Remains of the Day
The Republic
Therese Raquin
The Revenger's Tragedy
The Rime of the Ancient Mariner
The Road
The Rocking-Horse Winner
The Rover
The Sandman
The Satanic Verses
The Scarlet Ibis
The Scarlet Letter
The Scarlet Pimpernel
The School for Scandal
The Scorch Trials
The Seagull
The Second Sex
The Secret Life of Bees
The Secret River
The Shining
The Sign of the Four
The Snow Man
The Social Contract
The Sociological Imagination
The Sorrows of Young Werther
The Souls of Black Folk
The Sound and the Fury
The Sound of Waves
The Sovereignty and Goodness of God
The Spanish Tragedy
The Spirit Catches You and You Fall Down
The Steeple-Jack
The Story of My Life
The Storyteller
The Stranger
The Sun Also Rises
The Talented Mr. Ripley (Film)

Made in the USA
Middletown, DE
09 August 2025

11995830R00106